D0557558

Herbert Puchta
Mario Rinvolucri

Multiple Intelligences
in EFL

Exercises for secondary and adult students

HELBLING LANGUAGES
www.helblinglanguages.com

MULTIPLE INTELLIGENCES IN EFL
by Herbert Puchta and Mario Rinvolucri

All rights reserved; no part of this publication may be reproduced, stored in a retrieval system, or transmitted in any form or by any means, electronic, mechanical, photocopying, recording, or otherwise, without the prior written permission of the Publishers.

Photocopying of certain pages within this publication is permitted for classroom use, wherever indicated by the inclusion of the following sentence:

© HELBLING LANGUAGES 2005

ISBN 978-3-902504-25-8

First published 2005
9   8   7   6   5   4   3
2010   2009   2008   2007

Edited by Jane Arnold and Mari Carmen Fonseca
Copy edited by Caroline Petherick
Designed by Quantico
Cover design by Capolinea
Cover photos by Marka
Illustrations by Pietro Di Chiara

Printed by ✿ Grafica Veneta

Every effort has been made to trace the owners of any copyright material in this book. If notified, the publisher will be pleased to rectify any errors or omissions.

© Helbling Languages 2005. Please photocopy this page for use in class.

Dedication

We would like to dedicate this book to Howard Gardner without whose pioneering work this book would never have been written.

Herbert Puchta   Mario Rinvolucri

Acknowledgements

We would like to thank Howard Gardner for his positive feedback on the manuscript of this book and for his constructive criticism.

We would also like to express our apprecition to Lucia Astuti and Markus Spielmann for inviting us to publish this book with Helbling Languages. Thank you, too, to collagues at Pilgrims, Canterbury, and many colleagues in workshops around the world for helping us understand the Gardner framework better.

Mario would like to thank Bonnie Tsai for being an intellectual companion in pursuing the classroom implications of Howard Gardner's work and giving him useful information, intuitions and pointers.

Herbert would like to thank Günter Gerngross, his co-author of various coursebooks, for being a source of co-creativity for many years and for a lot of inspiration in applying the theory of multiple intelligences to EFL, and Edith Rainer for turning the manuscript from an amateur mess into a typographically polished whole.

Finally we would like to thank our editors, Jane Arnold and Mari Carmen Fonseca, for numerous useful comments on the original manuscript, and our desk editor, Caroline Petherick, for guiding the book through production.

Herbert and Mario

Bio-data

Herbert lives in a valley
He prioritises
He types at 80 words a minute
He writes coursebooks
He is amazed by people

Bio-data

Mario lives by the sea
He diversifies
He types at 35
He has forgotten what coursebooks are
He is amazed by people

He believes the student is hugeeguh si tneduts eht seveileb eH

They wrote siht koob

Contents

Contents

Introduction

If you want to find out what Multiple Intelligences are, read Section 1.
For a brief outline of the theory of Multiple Intelligences, read Section 2.
If your main question is: *What has this got to do with my teaching?*,
read Section 3.
If you want to understand how this book can help you develop your students'
thinking skills, read Section 4.
If you want to grasp the overall shape of the book, read Section 5.

Section 1:
What are Multiple Intelligences?

An influential idea that dominated 20th-century Western thinking was that
intelligence has two or perhaps three main strands: the logical–mathematical,
the linguistic and the spatial. This thinking was institutionalised in the standard
intelligence tests that were used in Western education to include some young
people and to exclude others (*page 24).

In the UK, for example, the 11+, a logical–mathematical, linguistic and spatial
test, was used to separate the "clever" 12-year-olds from the "dummies", so
that the 20% would go to grammar schools and the rest, the majority, to
secondary modern schools. This unhappy, socially divisive system still survives
today in the most politically conservative parts of the UK. In Chile in the 1970s,
university entrance depended on how well candidates did in Academic Aptitude
Tests, which had, at a higher level, a similar focus to the UK's 11+ test. Teachers
working in the Chilean university system came to think of a person with a test
score of 400 (OK for humanities) as being dim, and 650 (OK for medicine) as
being bright. In those years the dominant, narrow view of intelligence was not
only politically and institutionally accepted, but it was swallowed whole by many
teachers, including Herbert and Mario, the two authors of this book.

Howard Gardner's *Frames of Mind* (New York, 1983, Basic Books), came to
challenge the limited concept of intelligence outlined above. He proposed that
intelligence falls into the following seven areas:

1) The intrapersonal intelligence
When working in the mode of this intelligence, you focus on, and function in
terms of, self-knowledge, self-regulation, self-control. You are exercising your
meta-cognitive skills.

In this intelligence, the horizon is where the boundaries of self lie. This intelligence has to do with happiness at being on one's own, with joy at knowing oneself, with an awareness of one's own feelings and wishes. An ability to abstract oneself and to daydream is good evidence of the intrapersonal intelligence at work.

2) The interpersonal intelligence

Gardner writes:

> The core capacity here *is the ability to notice and make distinctions among other individuals* and, in particular, among their moods, temperaments and motivations and intentions. Examined in its most elementary form the interpersonal intelligence entails the capacity of the young child to discriminate among the individuals around him and to detect their various moods. Highly developed forms of this intelligence are to be found in religious and political leaders (as Mahatma Gandhi) in skilled parents and teachers, and in individuals enrolled in the helping professions, be they therapists, counsellors or shamans. (op. cit.)

Central to this intelligence is the ability to listen to what the other person seems to be saying (rather than to your distortion of it), to be able to gain good rapport with another person, and to be adept at negotiation and persuasion.

3) The logical–mathematical intelligence

Einstein, berated by his maths teachers for day-dreaming in class, wrote this about himself:

> I saw that mathematics was split up into numerous specialities, each of which could easily absorb the short lifetime granted to us. In physics, however, I soon learnt to sort out that which was able to lead to fundamentals and to turn aside from everything else, from the multitude of things that clutter up the mind and divert it from the essential. (op. cit.)

The above paragraph seems to provide a clear example of the logical–mathematical intelligence at work. Einstein uses few words to express broad ideas with sharp clarity. This intelligence can be associated with "scientific" thinking. It often comes into play in the analytical part of problem-solving – when we make connections and establish relationships between pieces of information that may seem separate, when we discover patterns, and when we are involved in planning, prioritising and systematising.

4) The linguistic intelligence

> By writing I was existing … my pen raced away so fast that often my wrists ached. I would throw the filled notebooks on the floor, I would eventually forget about them, they would disappear … I wrote in order to write. I didn't regret. Had I been read I would have tried to please.

I would have become a wonder again. Being clandestine, I was true. (op. cit.) Jean-Paul Sartre wrote these lines about himself at the age of nine, and in them he describes one aspect of the linguistic intelligence, an intelligence that is intensely concerned with form. His description also evokes the intrapersonal intelligence, in which other people are beyond the horizon. Can we invite you to do a small experiment? **Look at** and internally **listen to** these sentences, and see how much or how little you are intrigued by them:

> He's got this brilliant book on the brain.
>
> Inattention is quite likely to generate inner tension.
>
> I feel that five to one is grossly unfair.
>
> He wrote these lines about himself at the age of nine.
>
> Mary looked at John with nothing on.

For a person with a strong linguistic intelligence, ambiguity, and a tricky relationship between signifier and signified, can be exciting. You may chortle over a misprint like *univerity* for *university*. However, if the logical–mathematical aspect of your mind is dominant at the time of reading, you may find this kind of thing trivial or absurd. Logical–mathematical thinking is concerned with the content of sentences, while the linguistic state of mind revels in the relationship between form and content.

5) The musical intelligence

The following lines are taken from the MI Bill of Rights that you will find on page 45, and they express what a person with a strong musical intelligence may feel in a language class of the early 21st century:

> I want to find tunes for parts of each unit.
>
> I have a right to use my Walkman in the reading and writing parts of the lessons.
>
> Can we have more jazz chants?
>
> I want to sing the grammar.
>
> I have a right to listen to music that relaxes me.
>
> I have a right to listen to music that expresses my mood.
>
> I have a right to music to lighten my language work.

A person with a well-developed musical intelligence benefits from being in a world of beat, rhythm, tone, pitch, volume and directionality of sound.

Fortunately for us language teachers, many of these features are also properly part of our linguistic realm, though we can choose whether to emphasise them or not. In teaching those students who are strong in music, it makes sense to do so.

6) The spatial intelligence

Imagine yourself standing outside a large building that you know well, such as a theatre, swimming pool, mosque or leisure centre. Notice the relationship between the building and the space around it. Shut your eyes. *Mentally* enter the building, Stand stock still once you are inside, and notice what you can hear, and how the space you sense around you feels – the temperature, and the dryness or dampness of the place. Now mentally open your eyes and look around you. What lines do you notice? What colours? And what is the play of light and dark here and there within the space? (Gardner presents the spatial intelligence as being principally dependent on our ability to see, yet for some people perception of space can be through touch – as is the case for many blind people – through sound, the bat-like world of echo, and through somatic awareness. We maintain that perception of space is multi-sensory, even if, in many people, the visual aspect predominates.) If you have been able to follow the sensory instructions above easily and with pleasure, it seems that your spatial intelligence is functioning well!

Language uses spatial thinking when it describes time and other concepts in terms of space:

> *within three days*
> *in the space of two hours*
> *as long as you*
> *beyond the pale*
> *under no circumstances.*

It is arguable that space is the main metaphor area that is "wired into" language to explain a wide range of basic concepts. You would expect air-traffic controllers, architects, landscape gardeners, civil engineers and sculptors to have highly developed spatial awareness, as is clearly the case with Henry Moore:

> He thinks of the sculpture, whatever its size, as if he were holding it completely enclosed in the hollow of his hand; he mentally visualises a complete form from all around itself; he knows, while he looks at one side, what the other side is like; he identifies himself with its centre of gravity, its mass, its weight; he realises its volume, the space that the shape displaces in the air. (op. cit.)

7) The kinaesthetic bodily intelligence

Have you ever seen an Arab horseman on his mount, man and beast looking like one animal? The rider is in total harmony with his horse.

Have you ever seen a ten-year-old perform an Aikido *kata* of 50–60 movements, with crisp precision, smooth flow and not a single hesitation? Gardner suggests that:

> Characteristic of this intelligence is the ability to use one's body in highly differentiated and skilled ways, for expressive as well as goal-directed purposes: these we see as Marcel Marceau, the mime, pretends to run, climb or prop up a heavy suitcase. Characteristic as well is the capacity to work skilfully with objects, both those that involve the fine motor movements of one's fingers and hands and those that exploit gross motor movements of the body. (op. cit.)

Two "candidate" intelligences

Since the 1983 appearance of *Frames of Mind*, Gardner has gone on to propose two more possible intelligences, the *natural* intelligence and the *existential / spiritual* intelligence. The first of these two has to do with being in harmony with nature in the way that many early peoples were, and still are. Perhaps you have friends who know what should be done next in a garden, and then go and quietly do it? A half instinctive, half knowledge-based awareness of when to water, when not to water, when to manure, when to weed and when to leave undisturbed – all of these have to do with the natural intelligence.

When St Teresa of Avila writes:

> I live without living in myself
> And I die because I do not die

she is expressing something of the existential or spiritual intelligence. This intelligence has to do with perception of what is beyond, what is higher, what is greater than us. Maybe you have friends who go into certain spaces and sense something that they find hard to pin down and put into words. We have such a friend who resonates and is filled with something ineffable each time she enters certain churches.

When you reflect on the wealth of thinking experience that has been evoked in the last few pages, then it's clear that standard, reductionist intelligence tests seem grossly inadequate. Yet in most places they still hold political and institutional sway.

This book hopes to take its very small place in the struggle to get the many intelligences valued in society and in school. And in this book, we focus on our mutual area of special interest: the language classroom.

Section 2:
The theory of Multiple Intelligences

Some readers of *Section 1* may have been unsatisfied by the simple assertion that this or that set of behaviours, skills and beliefs constitute "an intelligence", without any attempt to define what an intelligence might be. What, for instance, could be done to evaluate claims that there is a "cooking", a "golfing", a "survival" or a "metaphorical" intelligence?

Howard Gardner proposes a number of criteria that would qualify a set of behaviours, skills and beliefs to be classified as a full-blown intelligence. Here are some of them:

1 *Brain damage may isolate a given intelligence and spare it, while destroying elsewhere*
We can speak of an intelligence being independent of other parts of the thinking apparatus if it's possible for a stroke or an accident to knock out other parts of the brain-mind but leave that original intelligence relatively intact. Independent existence of an intelligence can also be demonstrated if it's the neural infrastructure of a specific intelligence that is destroyed, leaving the rest of the brain unharmed. For example, damage to the motor cortex of the brain may leave a person paralysed, thus knocking out their capacity to express their body–kinaesthetic intelligence, while leaving the rest of the brain's thinking neurology still functioning.

2 *Each intelligence may well have its prodigies and/or "idiots savants"*
An "idiot savant" is a person who is precocious in one area but an idiot in everything else. The existence of such people shows that a given intelligence can operate at a high level and independently from the others.
In a case described by Lorna Selfe, we see a child with a highly developed spatial intelligence but a severe inability to be with other people, a serious deficit in her interpersonal intelligence. Nadia started drawing horses when she was three and a half years old – horses that looked like the work of a teenage artist. "She had a sense of space, an ability to depict appearances and shadows and a sense of perspective such as the most gifted child might

develop at three times her age." (*Nadia, a case of extraordinary drawing ability in an autistic child*, by Lorna Selfe, 1977, London Academic Press.) Bruno Bettelheim describes the case of Joey, the Mechanical Boy, whose one interest was in machines; he took them apart and put them together again, and he actually wanted to become a machine. When he came in for a meal, he laid down an imaginary wire, and connected himself to his source of electrical power. Joey lived entirely in his brilliant, kinaesthetic world of machines, but had come to work with Bettelheim because he was under-developed in every other area.

The case of Christopher, a linguistic idiot savant, is of particular interest, as it shows both the workings and the limitations of language intelligence. On a variety of logical–mathematical tests for which the average score is 100, Christopher scored 40–75. At the age of 20, his ability to draw people was about that of a six-year-old. Tests also showed that he had little notion of what was going on inside other people's minds; he and a five-year-old girl were shown one of her dolls hidden under a cushion of a settee, the girl was led out of the room, and the doll was then hidden behind a curtain. When Christopher was asked where, when she came back in, she would be likely to look for the doll, he suggested she would choose the *new* hiding place.

In the language area, however, Christopher was prodigiously able. He had some knowledge of and skill in using these tongues: Danish, Dutch, Finnish, French, German, Modern Greek, Hindi, Italian, Norwegian, Polish, Portuguese, Spanish, Turkish and Welsh.

He could learn from any source: a teach-yourself book, a grammar book, a native informant, etc.

He was happy with word games in any language he knew. When he was asked to take the German word *Regenschirm* (umbrella) and, using the letters of the original word, produce as many words in German as he could, he came up with these:

mein (my)

Schnee (snow)

Regen (rain)

Ich (I)

Schirm (screen, shelter, cover).

Christopher's case, documented in *The Mind of a Savant* (Neil Smith and Ianthi-Maria Tsimpli, 1995, Basil Blackwell, Oxford) is particularly interesting in that it shows how limited the language intelligence is on its own, without any power in other areas of thinking. The boy was given an English text to translate into three other languages. He did the task fast and "linguistically" well – while completely failing to notice that the original was syntactically fractured and did not make sense. Any person operating logically, or at any rate more holistically, would have declared the task impossible.

3 *An intelligence will have a core set of operations*

These core operations are triggered by stimuli coming in from outside, or arising within, at a certain point in a person's development. An example of this would be initial sensitivity to the relationship between different pitches, given that dealing with pitch is one of the core functions of the musical intelligence. Another example of a core operation would be the ability to imitate body movement, one of the core operations of kinaesthetic intelligence.

4 *An intelligence will have a developmental process or history*

Each intelligence will develop in identifiable steps as the person goes from the womb to adulthood. There may well be critical periods during which development speeds up. If the appropriate stimuli are absent during such periods, then development may be stunted.

5 *An intelligence will tend to be encodable in a symbolic system*

Drawing serves as a notational system for the spatial intelligence. Music can be written on the page, and has given rise to several notational systems. Language is principally a code: a primary oral one and a secondary written one, sign language being a kinaesthetic–visual code. Mathematics has whole sets of symbolic systems embodying it. Ballet scenarii can be symbolically represented on the page, an encoding of one aspect of the body–kinaesthetic intelligence. Of the seven intelligences that Gardner put forward in his 1983 book (op. cit.), only the intrapersonal and interpersonal intelligences are beyond the scope of any attempt to encode in a symbolic system.

Though the above list of criteria for an intelligence is not a complete one, enough has been said to give some idea of how Gardner defines "an intelligence". As neurology invents better tools for tracking what is physically going on in the brain, we are likely to get more evidence about how each intelligence functions chemically and electrically.

Though it is useful for analytical clarity to speak separately of different intelligences, in daily life we frequently use several intelligences simultaneously. When a person opens their personal diary to write about a meeting they've had with a colleague, they are typically alone in the room and writing for themselves. Their diary is a form of inner monologue exteriorised onto paper, and their intrapersonal intelligence is in play. As they write, they may speculate about the meeting from the other person's point of view, so engaging their interpersonal intelligence. As the expression of all this is through language they are clearly also exercising their linguistic intelligence.

We feel it is actually rare for a person to be involved exclusively in the exercise of only one of their intelligences. For example, as Mario writes these lines of explanatory text he is using his logical-mathematical intelligence to marshal his ideas and sequence them, his language intelligence to express them in English, and his interpersonal ability to try and gauge their effect on the reader.

Section 3:
Multiple intelligences in your classroom

Good teachers are usually enthusiastic about their subject. However, they often find their students don't share their enthusiasm. For example, it has been said that only one out of five language teachers were good at maths when they were themselves pupils at school. If you had been in the other four-fifths – and even if you had been lucky enough to have had an enthusiastic, inspiring teacher – this might not have been enough to make maths comprehensible and attractive to you. Yet, had those who had been poor at maths had a teacher like Mark Wahl to make it attainable and available to people who were weak logically–mathematically but who were rich in other intelligences, then maybe it would have become open to them, too. Here is what Wahl says in his book, *Math for Humans*, about the way he helped a visually–spatially intelligent second-grade girl take her first steps towards coping with arithmetic:

> I asked her to make a picture incorporating 8+7=15 and to do this on a large index card. I asked her to paint four more cards with other math facts on them. When she came back each card was a painting in which could be discerned the symbols of a math equation creating the outline of trees, person, beach towels etc. I looked at her first card and asked her:
> 'How much is 8+7?'
> Silence. Then I said:

'It's the beach scene,' and she immediately said: '15'.

She ended with a deck of artistic flashcards that soon created answer associations for her without my having to provide scene clues. My logical–mathematical intelligence could never figure out how her mind did this, but there was no need to – she was successful with her facts and her math performance too, thanks to her spatial intelligence.

This teacher had sufficient respect for the girl's strengths beyond and outside mathematical thinking to teach her in a way that, in the long run, helped her make sense of the maths problems he set her. He drew her into her logical–mathematical intelligence via her spatial ability.

We feel that you can work just as Wahl did, if you are prepared to systematically involve other intelligence areas in your language lessons.
If you do this you can expect enrichment in a number of areas:

- Your students' motivation depends partly on how "addressed" they feel in your class and on how meaningful they think the activities in your class are to them. If your teaching focus is on the linguistic domain only, you will get excellent results with the minority of students who are strong in this area. If, however, you regularly use exercises like the ones suggested in this book, you will notice that students whose strengths lie in areas other than the linguistic one will activate themselves more and will develop an interest in your subject and want to find out more about it.
- Generally speaking, we tend to regard as intelligent those students who show a high degree of linguistic ability and who therefore share the intelligence that language teachers are strong in. If the focus of your teaching is mainly on the activation of the language intelligence, students whose strong areas are elsewhere may easily be seen by you as inactive, stupid and demotivated. Using activities that draw on a variety of intelligences will help you to better appreciate the strengths, otherwise hidden, of these students. Consequently they will feel more appreciated by you and will feel better about what they achieve in the foreign-language class.
- Although you can never predict what kind of thought process a certain activity will trigger in your students' minds, it is safe for us to claim that using activities like the ones in this book is likely to activate a wider range of intelligences than if you taught language purely "linguistically".
As students gradually realise that they can approach language from their strength areas, they will feel better in the language class and may become

more willing to take risks and begin to develop areas that are not "their own". So you may begin to find it possible to involve students in discussion of perceived cognitive weaknesses and strengths, thus contributing to the students' meta-cognitive awareness – thinking about their own thinking – which is a useful step in mental development.

Let us now show you an example of teaching a language area multi-intelligently. The topic of the lesson was punctuation, and the target group were 13-year-olds. The teacher split them into groups of six, and gave each group a different reading passage, each consisting of two short paragraphs. They were given 10–15 minutes to work on the texts, and to work up a percussion system in which they agreed on specific sounds and/or actions to replace the punctuation marks. In each group, a learner then read the passage aloud, pausing at each punctuation mark, while the other five made the specific sound and/or did the specific action. For example:

The girl looked down, "I love you"

Reader: **The girl looked down**
The group of five snapped their fingers in unison once, to represent the comma.
The group clapped their hands once, to represent opening inverted commas.
Reader: **I love you**
The group clapped their hands twice to represent closing inverted commas.

This activity helped the children realise that punctuation is more than random salt and pepper on the page, and it did this by appealing to their musical, kinaesthetic and interpersonal intelligences. The exercise outlined is much more effective than lengthy explanations by the teacher about the function of each punctuation mark.

(For more on this exercise see page 81. Our first experience of it was at the **University of the First Age,** in Birmingham, UK, a programme imbued with MI thinking and aimed at poor children of the city's ghettos.)

Another exercise that focuses on punctuation and appeals to students' interpersonal intelligence is when lower intermediate students are asked to write short letters to each other while role-playing punctuation marks.
Let's say Laszlo, a Hungarian student, decides to write to Ana, a classmate from

Argentina, who he decides to characterise as an exclamation mark. His letter might start:

Dear !,
I am writing to tell you that I find it amazing that you are able to say something so strongly, so clearly, when you speak to other people. No, not ...
I do not mean your English. I mean the way you express your thoughts, your feelings ...

What might seem at first like a rather strange exercise can, when done with a warmed-up, intermediate class of older teenagers or adults, have interesting results. What are students doing as they write such letters? In the first place they are expressing new things about their partner via the metaphor, and secondly they are doing an in-depth exploration of how they understand and use this punctuation mark. (For a fuller outline of this activity, see *Letters*, Burbidge *et al*, 1996, OUP.)

"But I guess I've been using multiple intelligences in my teaching for years!" we hear you say.

You are right – and you are right in at least two distinct ways:
• You have been offering MI stimuli to the students. For example, when a teacher, drawing on *Drama Techniques in Language Teaching* (Maley and Duff, 1978, CUP), gets students doing activities such as Hotel Receptionist, in which a volunteer mimes a sentence that the other students have to guess and have to recreate, word-for-word accurately, the appeal is equally to the kinaesthetic and to the linguistic intelligences.
• Quite independently of your intentions, your students have been freely using their intelligences in multiple ways in your classroom. In this sense, your classroom has inevitably been full of MI work.

This book offers you now a choice of activities to enable you to invite your students to use their strongest intelligences as well as develop the weaker ones. We wish to stress the fact that the activities offer invitations rather than being mono-directional "single-intelligence exercises". Whatever intelligence we invite our students into, we can be sure that there will always be people in our class who will instinctively process the invitation in ways different from the ones we would have predicted they would use. These intriguing differences in the way the human brain works can become stimuli for discussions of individual thinking processes, and learning from each other.

To illustrate our point, let's take an activity that many people would reasonably regard as an essentially musical one, and let us notice the very varied ways in which students executed the task that was set for them:

> The students stand up and spread out around the space available so there is plenty of room round them. They shut their eyes. They imagine an orchestra in front of them and they mentally become the conductor. They are asked to lead the orchestra through a three-minute snatch of music. If they don't like classical music, they can choose to be a band leader, a pop star or whatever.

From one class we had this feedback:

I couldn't hear any music but something was vibrating through my body.
I was in movement and flow (kinaesthetic processing).
I just heard music from somewhere up above me … no need to move at all (musical and spatial thinking).
Yes, there was music in the background, but I was really aware of myself, my body and my breathing (intrapersonal mode, and also musical and kinaesthetic).
The violins were the problem … we were rehearsing and I just could not get them to come in at the right time. I don't think they liked me (interpersonal).
I was in a high mountain valley and there was snow on some of the mountains. I knew I had to get across this torrent but could see no bridge (visual–spatial).
My mind went totally blank … I don't know what I did for those long minutes.

To get as much as possible out of the activities in the book, it may well be worth you allowing time for the students to tell each other about their inner processes, as happened in the lesson above. The outcomes of the activities may often go beyond the realms of the intelligence areas you have invited your students to work in, so some of their reactions may surprise and delight you!

Section 4:
Developing thinking skills through MI work

The principal aim of this book is to bring the richness of MI thinking to EFL students, and so to speed up, deepen and generally enhance their learning process.

People learn language much better when allowed to do so within the wide range of perspectives afforded by MI. But there is another significant benefit of using the activities in this book – the development of a range of cross-curricular thinking skills that go beyond the language classroom to become a positive force for improving your students' lives in general.

To illustrate this, we would like to analyse three activities from the book, enumerating the thinking and feeling skills that these exercises can develop in your students:

The Prototype exercise on page 54 asks students to decide how close they consider a variety of bird types – eagle, humming-bird, hen, sparrow, etc – are to the prototypical idea of 'Bird'. From a language-teaching point of view, the point of the exercise is to teach or revise a lexical set in an interesting way that draws on logical–mathematical skills.

But the students are working simultaneously on the question of the extent to which a member of a set belongs to that set: for example, how fully do mermaid, foetus, centaur and lunatic belong to the set 'Human'? This kind of logical–mathematical activity helps to develop thinking skills that will be of use in other subjects that have nothing to do with language work.

In the area of, for example, art criticism, prototype thinking can be applied in this way: How far and to what extent do these artists fully belong to the set 'Painter': a cartoonist, a water-colourist, Rembrandt, Matisse, a graffiti-sprayer, etc. The exercise leads the budding art critic to define just what they understand the term "painter" to essentially mean. What for them, and there will be creative disagreement, is the prototypal core meaning of "painter"?

Let's look at a second activity, Human Camera on page 114. In this exercise, students walk around in pairs, student A with her hands on B's shoulders. B walks along with her eyes shut; B is A´s camera. When A presses B´s shoulder, B opens her eyes for a count of three and 'takes a photograph' of what she sees in front of her, i.e. she commits the scene to memory. A uses B to take three photos, and then they swap roles to repeat the exercise.

The language element of this exercise is the verbalising of mental pictures – but the core skills being practised here are the accurate visual perception of the scene and the committing of it to medium-term memory. These kinds of mental skills are needed by photographers, architects, designers, website creators and many others. Your students will develop these skills – vital ones in some subject areas – without being aware that this is what they are doing; and so they are engaged in powerful peripheral learning.

The Human Camera activity also helps people to take tests more confidently – irrespective of the subject area. We know that students with an inborn talent for visualisation tend to do better in exams. There are even students with eidetic ability, who can call up to mind whole pages of their textbooks as they set about answering their exam questions. Human Camera provides an enjoyable way to help students develop their ability to visualise and to remember what they have seen, and thus often achieve higher marks.

The third exercise we would like to focus your attention on is Positive Language Learning Affirmations, page 150. This activity aims to help students to move from an "I can't do it" state of mind towards one in which they have trust in their own abilities. The students repeat, and take on board, positive statements about themselves when these are given to them by the teacher, and they also create some positive statements of their own.

The reason for asking students to internalise a set of positive self-statements is that many of our more diffident students, who do not believe in their own ability, continually run active and negative inner-voice programs through which they put themselves down as thoroughly as possible, saying over and over again:

"I don't think I can manage …"
"I've never done well at….."
"I'm just no good at …."

As Jane Arnold* says, 'Many learners, especially low-achievers, have been strongly affected by years of negative self-talk, much of it on a semi-unconscious level.'

The positive affirmations that students develop in the exercise described above serve as guardian angels to fight off these hidden, sometimes self-created, inner demons.

The exercise aims to combat the creation and maintenance of a destructive self-image in connection with learning English, but works equally well for any other subject.

In a way, this third activity condenses into just one and half pages the whole philosophy of this book:

'I can do well in this subject if I bring my strengths to it ... I can!'

* Arnold J (Ed.) (1999) Affect in Language Learning Cambridge: Cambridge University Press, p. 17

Section 5:
The shape of this book

If you are currently working from coursebooks, you might first turn to Chapter 2. Here you will find exercises designed to fit in with the material in the units you are already teaching.

This chapter also floats the sensible idea that you do not need to plod sequentially through the coursebook: there may be a strong case for using exercises that go back to units already worked on, and forward to units you will cover in depth in some weeks' time.

You may be teaching the same material through for the second, third, etc. time. So you may find that, though the students coming fresh to the book are happy with it, you will be starting to stifle your yawns! In this situation, the activities in Chapter 2 will allow you to brighten up your teaching hours without deviating from the line and content of the textbook.

If you want to achieve a firmer idea of how the intelligences work, turn to Chapter 1, General MI Exercises You might want to read Section 1 of this introduction and then try out a couple of exercises from Chapter 1 with family or friends. You might choose one of these:

The intelligences on holiday (page 41).
Get to know the group via MI (page 48).
The MI Bill of Rights (page 44).

In Chapter 3 you have a spread of exercises that invite learners to work in their interpersonal intelligences. These communicative activities are of a sort you are probably familiar with from many Teacher Resource Books.

Chapter 4 offers you exercises that will appeal to the more introspective learners, to the people who sigh a little when asked, yet again, to work in pairs! Here is something for students with a strong intrapersonal need. We feel there has been a lack of this kind of inward-focused activity, in which a person is left to work on language without prying, supervision, or the demand that they communicate with others. A few unit titles will give you a flavour of Chapter 4:

Imaging
   Listening with your mind's eye
   Concentration on language
   Intrapersonal questionnaires
   Inner grammar games.

The final part of the book, Chapter 5, Self-Management, is rather more demanding of you and the students than the lesson outlines that have been given in the earlier sections. The ideas in this chapter will work best in groups that are well warmed up and in which a reasonable climate of trust has developed.

FUN is central to the whole idea of this book. We agree with the poet Schiller – and we agree with rats! It was Schiller who said that you are only human insofar as you can play, and you can only play insofar as you are human. Recent research on rats has shown that after a boring day rats experience very little memory-consolidating sleep, while after a day in a stimulating environment, they do lots of memory-fixing sleep. Is it really necessary to go to experimental neurology or to the giants of German literature to substantiate the claim that fun is central to efficient learning? It seems obvious!

* The Stanford–Binet Intelligence Scale is a direct descendant of the Binet–Simon Scale, the first ever intelligence scale, created in 1905 by Alfred Binet and Theophilus Simon.

The Stanford–Binet Scale tests intelligence across four areas:
- verbal reasoning
- quantitative reasoning
- abstract/visual reasoning
- short-term memory.

The areas are covered by 15 subtests, including those on:
- vocabulary
- comprehension
- verbal absurdities
- pattern analysis
- matrices
- paper-folding and paper-cutting
- copying
- quantitative ability
- number series
- equation building
- memory for sentences
- memory for digits
- memory for objects
- bead memory.

(The above quotation comes from: www.healthatoz.com/healthatoz/Atoz/ency/stanford-binet_intelligence_scales.jsp)

CHAPTER 1
GENERAL MI EXERCISES

Introducing a person through Multiple Intelligences

Language focus	Description, evaluation, and the vocabulary associated with the MIs
Proposed MI focus	All
Level	Lower intermediate to advanced
Time	Lesson 1: 50 minutes Lesson 2: 50 minutes
Preparation	Have a list of the intelligence domains, including "closeness to the elements and to nature".

Mentally prepare to show the class a person you know very well by "becoming" this person. You need to be able to sit like this person at a table, to sit like them in an easy chair, to stand and walk like them maybe to run/swim/bike/drive/dance etc.

Prepare to describe this person's style of dress. Prepare to use your voice in the sort of way this person does: do they speak slow or fast – do they speak high or low – do they speak continuously or do they pause a lot?

Also prepare to speak about this person's relationship to the world of music – be ready to speak *as* them, using the first person.

in class

Lesson 1

1 Ask the students to get up and move around the room to find a partner, perhaps one they do not normally work with. Explain that this will be a pairing over two lessons.

2 Explain that you want the A's in each pair to think of a person they know well, and to prepare to "become" them. Demonstrate what you mean, by "becoming" the person you have chosen.

List all the intelligence domains on the board. Explain that you want the A's then to talk about their person's skills and awareness in each of the intelligence domains.

Demonstrate by speaking in the first person, by sitting as "your" person would sit, and by using their sort of voice. Speak about "your" musical experiences, in role.

3 Ask the A's to sit with their partners and go into their role, showing the B's how their person sits, drives, walks etc. Ask the A's, now *being* their person, to describe their musical awareness and skills, and their spatial abilities. And then to describe some experiences which explain how they relate to others, and how they feel inside themselves, when they're on their own etc. Tell them they have half an hour for the role-play.

4 Have a brief feedback session about how the A's felt in their role.

Lesson 2
The B's get the chance to do what the A's did in Lesson 1.
Allow time for a longer wind-up and feedback session at the end.

2 Who has helped me with my intelligences?

Language focus	Writing
Proposed MI focus	Intrapersonal and interpersonal
Level	Lower intermediate to advanced
Time	30–40 minutes
Preparation	Copy the worksheet (page 29), one for each student.

in class

1 Give out the worksheets and ask the students to go through them on their own.
2 Put the students in groups and ask them to discuss what has come up from working through the worksheets.
3 Round off with a plenary discussion.

MI Worksheet

The best known people displaying the various types of intelligence are:

Logical–mathematical	Albert Einstein
Musical	Wolfgang Amadeus Mozart
Kinaesthetic	Rudolph Nureyev
Linguistic	William Shakespeare
Intrapersonal	Diogenes
Spatial	Leonardo da Vinci
Interpersonal	Mahatma Gandhi

People also talk of:
Natural intelligence - being in harmony with the weather, the seasons, plant growth, animals etc.

Put the relevant intelligences in the gaps below, and in the lines below jot down words that come to mind as you think of those memories:

When I was a child I was naturally strong in the _____ intelligence(s).

_____
_____
_____
_____

Between 5 and 10 years old I was encouraged in the _____ intelligence(s).

_____
_____
_____
_____

When I was a child I felt less strong in _____ intelligence(s).

_____
_____
_____
_____

Now I feel strong in the _____ intelligence(s).

_____
_____
_____
_____

© Helbling Languages 2005. Please photocopy this page for use in class.

From music to sculpture

Language focus	Writing
Proposed MI focus	Musical and kinaesthetic
Level	Lower intermediate to advanced
Time	40–50 minutes
Preparation	Choose a piece of music appropriate to the age group, to last 2–4 minutes. It should be a piece they are unlikely to know already.

in class

1 To get the students into a calm mood, ask them to shut their eyes and measure a minute any way they like except by looking at their watch or a clock. Tell them to say "minute" or "end" when they reckon their minute is up, but to keep their eyes shut.

2 Ask them to keep their eyes shut, and then play them the piece of music you have selected.

3 When the music has ended, ask each student to write a paragraph about the pictures they saw as they listened, the smells they experienced, the feelings they had, the day-dream they went into or the thoughts that came to them.

4 Group the students into fours to share their paragraphs.

5 Ask each group to prepare a human "sculpture" that represents their feeling about the music. They need to include all four people in the sculpture and to take up a position they can hold for 10 to 15 seconds.

6 Each group shows their sculpture to the rest of the class.

7 Each student writes a paragraph about each of the sculptures.

8 Ask the students to stick the paragraphs up round the walls, so people can go and read each other's.

Acknowledgement
We have modified an idea that we learnt from Gill Johnson.

Language tricks

Language focus	Phrasing, intonation, assimilation, punctuation and syntax
Proposed MI focus	Linguistic and logical–mathematical
Level	Intermediate to advanced
Time	30–40 minutes
Preparation	None.

in class

1 Get the students' attention and then tell them this riddle:

There were twenty six sheep in field. One died. How many left?

(When you say it, be sure to run "six" and "sheep" together, so that the sentence could equally well be heard as: "There were twenty *sick* sheep in a field.")

Be ready to accept all thoughtful answers – write them up on the board. In the past, students have given us these answers:

- 25 walked out of the field – one was dead
- there were 25 left alive
- there were 26 left – the dead one was still there
- one dyed – so there were 26 sheep, but one was a different colour.

If your students find it hard to see the second meaning of the sentence, give them a clue. Tell them another good answer is 19. Ask them to work out how this can be so.

2 Write this word string on the board. Ask the students to punctuate it so that it makes good sense:

I think that that that that that student has written is wrong.

Ask them to work with a partner to find the solution.
(Solution: *I think that that "that" that that student wrote is wrong.* When you read the sentence, pronounce the first and the fourth "that" with a short schwa, emphasize the third, and pause after it.)

3 Write this word string on the board, and ask the students to punctuate it and to add one word:

I think that the Fish and and and Chips are too apart on this sign.

They work in pairs.
(Solution: *I think that the "Fish" and "and" and "Chips" are too far apart on this sign.*)

4 Give the student this string and ask them what order the numbers are in:

8   5   4   9   1   7   6   10   3   2
(Solution: alphabetical order of the words for the numbers.)

5 Finally give the students this string to punctuate for homework:

Peter where Mary had had had had had had had had had had the teacher's approval.
(Solution: This was a language test: *Peter, where Mary had had "had had", had had "had". "Had had" had the teacher's approval.*)

5 Turning a verse inside out

Language focus	Sounds and their spellings, the rhythm of language
Proposed MI focus	Linguistic and musical
Level	Post-beginner to advanced
Time	15–20 minutes with an advanced class 40 minutes with a post-beginner one
Preparation	Have this nursery rhyme ready in your head:

> *Jack and Jill went up the hill*
> *To fetch a pail of water.*
> *Jack fell down and broke his crown*
> *And Jill came tumbling after.*

in class

1 Put the rhyme up on the board and read it to the class twice. Explain any unknown words. Ask the students to choral-read the lines several times.

2 Rub out a couple of words in different parts of the rhyme and ask a student to read the four lines, including the rubbed-out words. Keep on rubbing out different words and getting different students to read the full text each time, till the board is blank and the class knows the rhyme. (Check that no one has written the text in their notebooks!)

This phase allows you to do plenty of useful phonological correction by simply pointing to the things that have been read wrong and asking for a better reading. You can do this effectively without opening your mouth.

3 Ask one student to act as the class secretary. Get the students to dictate the poem to him/her, but with the words in each line spoken in reverse order, like this:

> *Hill the up went Jill and Jack*
> *Water of pail a fetch to… etc.*

They all recite the backwards poem together. (Then you erase it.)

4 Get the whole class to recite the verse, starting with the last line and ending with the first:

> *And Jill came tumbling after*
> *Jack fell down and broke his crown…etc.*

Turning a verse inside out

5 Get a new secretary up to the board. The class dictates the spelling of the verse to the secretary but replaces all the vowels with whistles. The secretary leaves a blank for each whistle.

6 Lead the class in reciting the poem:
- whispering
- softly but with voice
- with lips moving but no sound
- singing
- using a different English accent
  (e.g. American if you normally offer a UK model.)
- speaking in a strong mother-tongue accent.

Acknowledgement
This a curtailed version of the 33-step auditory-visual exercise to be found in *On Love and Psychological Exercises*, A. R. Orage, 1998, Samuel Weiser.

6 Which meaning?

Language focus	Sentence-level ambiguity
Proposed MI focus	Linguistic intelligence
Level	Intermediate to advanced
Time	40–50 minutes
Preparation	None.

in class

1 Explain to the students that you are going to give them the first sentence of a paragraph. Their task is, working individually, to complete the paragraph by inventing two more sentences. DO NOT tell them that the sentences you will be giving them are ambiguous.

2 Dictate the first sentence:

I had a row with David over Christmas.
("over" can mean "about", or can indicate the period of time)

Then allow time for them to write their complete paragraph.

Here are seven more paragraph head-sentences:

We have to get three down.
(Could be a crossword puzzle, could be boxes, could be ideas or words you are copying.)

GIANT WAVES DOWN TUNNEL
(This could refer to a giant who's waving – or to big waves of water.)

Read the next sentence with "neutral" intonation:
I don't like a lot of people.
(Does the writer dislike crowds – or is the writer a misanthrope?)

The stewardess ticked off the passengers as they boarded the aircraft.
(She ticked them off on a list – or she reprimanded them.)

The vet decided to operate on the cow's inside.
(Could also be understood as: The vet decided to operate on the cows inside.)

Actually, it's five to six.
(5.55 – or from five o'clock till six o'clock)

I think we've asked an awful lot of them.
(Have we been too demanding – or have we invited too many people?)

3 Group the students into fours and ask them to compare their paragraphs. As they compare, they will find out for themselves that some of them may have understood the head-sentence differently from the way their classmates did.

4 Run through the sentences to make sure that all the ambiguities are made clear to the students.

Variation

Ask the students to write down your ambiguous sentence, and imagine the scene it brings to mind. They then each draw a quick sketch of what they have imagined. The language work happens when they get together and explain their drawings to one another.

Note

You will find more ambiguous sentences in *Dictation*, Davis, 1989, CUP, and *More Grammar Games*, Davis, 1995, CUP, though the exercise frame offered there is different from the one above.

7

Knowing by heart

Language focus	Internalising a stretch of FL text
Proposed MI focus	Intrapersonal and kinaesthetic
Level	Beginner to advanced (also useful in primary)
Time	Lesson 1: 2 minutes Lesson 2: 10–15 minutes (depending on length of text.)
Preparation	Choose and copy a text you want them to memorise. Make one copy per student and five more.

in class

Lesson 1

Give out the text and ask them to learn it by heart for homework.

Lesson 2

1 Put five copies of the text up along the front wall of the classroom and ask all the students to come to the front of the room.

2 The students turn their backs on the text and walk slowly back across the room, reciting the text as they go, *sotto voce*. If there is a bit they can't remember, they go back to the front and re-read that bit.

3 The exercise is over when most of the students have reached the back wall, having successfully recited the whole text.

Note

Some outstanding language learners opt to learn short texts in the target language by heart. Learning by heart is the method favoured by traditional educational systems, such as those in Islamic countries and in China.

Antoine de la Garanderie suggests that taking in text uncritically and committing it to memory is one the four principal ways in which humans learn (For more on this, see *Ways of Doing*, Davis *et al*, 1999, Cambridge, pages 122–124.)

In Gardner's terms, learning by heart is a major intrapersonal way of coming to grips with a foreign language. This exercise partly socialises this intrapersonal work, as the students recite the text at their own pace and to themselves but with others round them.

Acknowledgement

We learnt this technique from Stephan Hegglin, a Swiss state-school teacher who often carries out science experiments in his English class.

The specialised autobiographies of my intelligences

Language focus	Past-tense verb forms
Proposed MI focus	The intelligence you choose to deal with, plus intrapersonal and interpersonal. In this activity the first type of intelligence tackled is the kinaesthetic
Level	Intermediate to advanced
Time	Lesson 1: 40–50 minutes Lesson 2: 40–50 minutes
Preparation	None.

in class

Lesson 1

1 Dictate the following set of questions:
  - How did different people cuddle me when I was little?
  - What were the first difficult things I can remember doing with my hands when I was very little?
  - Did I have problems with buttons or shoe laces or things inside out and back-to-front?
  - What were my first songs with movements at home and at school?
  - What memories come back of my first skiing, swimming or bike riding?
  - When and where did I first dance?
  - Have I learnt any new ways of dancing in the last few years?
  - How many different ways have I swum, in how many different places, and in how many different temperatures?
  - Which activities do I do in which a sense of balance is important?
  - What are the three most complicated things I am able to do with my hands today?
  - Which are my favourite gestures, and are they the same as those of others in my family?
  - Do I have to write words out to be sure of how to spell them?
  - What activities have I experienced where awareness of the movements of others is enjoyable?

2 Group the students in threes and ask them to answer and discuss the questions.

Lesson 2

1 Remind the students of the above lesson on their kinaesthetic history.

Explain that they are going to choose another intelligence to work on, and offer them either *musical* or *logical–mathematical* or *intrapersonal*.

Get them to divide into three groups according to the area they want to work on. Within these groups get them to work in threes or fours.

In each small group one person is the interviewee, and the others interview them about their past experiences in this intelligence.

2 Make sure that as many people as possible get the chance to be interviewed.

Sequence in a story

Language focus	Writing paragraphs for a newspaper-style story
Proposed MI focus	Logical–mathematical, interpersonal
Level	Upper intermediate
Time	30–40 minutes
Preparation	Photocopy the whole story (page 40), one copy for each student.

Also, for every 10 students in your class you will need to make one copy of each of the last five paragraphs, and cut them up separately.

in class

1 Ask the students to work in pairs and give each pair one of the paragraphs numbered 1 to 5.

Tell the pairs that you have given them a paragraph taken from somewhere in a news story. Ask them to write the paragraph they think precedes it and the one that follows it. Tell them not to use more than 30 words in either paragraph, and not less than 20. Tell them to call you if they need language help.

2 If you have 10 students in class, get them to group together. The pair with paragraph **3** reads their original paragraph first, and then the preceding and following paragraphs that they have written.

They repeat the same process with the pairs who have paragraphs **1**, **4**, **5** and **2**, in that order.

If you have 20 students in your class, then have two groups working simultaneously; if 30 students, three groups etc.

3 Hand out copies of the complete story. Ask the learners to read the paragraphs in the order of the original news story.

4 Allow time for their comments on how news stories are written.

Note
The story is typical of the "inverted pyramid" of the agency-style news story. The headline and the first paragraphs are packed with information and give "the big picture". The subsequent paragraphs go into more, and less essential, detail.

6 **Gunmen shoot man in head after robbery**

7 A businessman was robbed and shot in the head on the doorstep of his secluded home, police said yesterday.

3 Trevor Shine, 40, who holds joint British-American citizenship, was said last night to be comfortable after an emergency operation to remove a bullet from his head.

1 He was attacked after he answered the door of his home in Brookwood, near Woking, Surrey, to two men at about 9.00 pm on Wednesday.

4 They each produced a gun and robbed him of his credit cards and cash before shooting him in the head and arm as they left.

5 Det. Insp. Phil Waters of Surrey Police said: "There is no indication as to why he was shot but he has had a miraculous escape. They certainly intended to kill him."

2 Mr Shine, who is believed to be a director of a market research company in Teddington, South West London, managed to call for help after the raid and was taken to hospital, where his wife, Melanie, was last night by his side. She and her baby daughter were out at the time of the robbery.

(Friday 3 Dec, 1999, the *Daily Telegraph*, page 5)

© Helbling Languages 2005. Please photocopy this page for use in class.

10 The intelligences on holiday

Language focus	Speaking
Proposed MI focus	All
Level	Intermediate
Time	30–40 minutes
Preparation	None.

in class

1 Ask the students to think back to a holiday away from home that they really enjoyed.

Dictate these questions to the students:
- Where were you?
- How long was the holiday?
- Who were you with?
- What kind of light was there?
- What weather did you have?
- What temperature was it?
- What new sounds do you remember hearing?
- Did you see anything you'd never seen before?

2 The students work in fours to answer the questions they have written down.

3 Dictate this second questionnaire to the students:
- What kind of space did you live in?
- Did the space you were in feel or look different to you when you came back to it again after you had been away from it?
- Was the place you were in easy or complicated to learn about and get accustomed to?
- What tunes, lyrics or music did you take with you in your head on the holiday?
- What musical experiences did you have while there?
- What would your body say about the time spent there, if you asked it?
- Which were the best conversations you had with yourself?
- What was the best time you spent on your own?
- Did any problems arise that you thought through successfully?
- Which numbers were important while you were away?
- Who were the most intriguing and or friendly people you came across or were with?
- When do you reckon you thought and spoke most fluently and fully?
- Were there any moments when you felt really in harmony with the sky and the land and the place itself?

4 The students go back to their fours and answer the questions.

Note

The "reflective dictation" format proposed above is particularly good at bringing out the students' thoughts and feelings. The dictation phase allows them to realise their own thoughts intrapersonally before they have the problem of expressing them to others in English.

Contradiction

Language focus	The apparent meaning versus implicit meanings
Proposed MI focus	Logical–mathematical
Level	Advanced
Time	20–30 minutes
Preparation	None.

in class

1 Write this sentence on the board:

There are no adjectives in this short sentence.

Wait for the class to react. The word "short" is an adjective, so clearly the sentence contradicts itself, as does this one:

There aren't any negatives on this line.

2 Ask the students to use a piece of paper turned sideways, to landscape, and draw three wide columns on it. They head the first column CONTRADICTORY and the second column I'M NOT SURE and the third column COHERENT.

Ask them to take down the sentences you dictate, putting them in the column they believe to be the appropriate one.

- This sentence ends with a noun.*
- This sentence is in my handwriting.*
- And don't start sentences with a conjunction.
- Never use a long word where a diminutive one will do.
- My handwriting is beautifully legible.*
- If any verb is improper at the end of sentence, a linking verb is.
- Don't you never go using double negatives, now, will you?
- This dictation will stop at the end of this sentence.*
- Unqualified superlatives are the worst of all.
- Avoid putting statements in the negative form.

(The sentences marked with * are, or may be, true. The last sentence is hard to categorise: "avoid" has a negative meaning, but the sentence is not grammatically negative.)

3 Ask the students to work in threes, and compare their categorisation of the sentences.

MI Bill of Rights

Language focus	Reading and discussing
Proposed MI focus	All
Level	Intermediate
Time	20–40 minutes
Preparation	Copy one "Bill of Rights" for every pair of students (see pages 45-47).

in class

1 Put the students into pairs. Ask them to read through the whole text of the Bill of Rights, and then write two more Rights of their own in each section that speak to them.

They don't need to do this for sections that they are not in sympathy with.

2 Pass seven blank OHP transparencies (one for each section of the Bill) around the class, and ask each pair to write their two new Rights onto the relevant sheets.

3 Put up the seven transparencies, and in each case ask the students which are the three or four most important Rights for them. Also give them a chance to say which sections don't appeal to them and why.

(For a future lesson with another class, use the Bill of Rights that's been produced by these students – what they have produced will most likely be more relevant than what we show in the example.)

Acknowledgement

The strategic idea of getting students in class A to prepare materials for students in class B comes from Sheelagh Deller's seminal book *Lessons from the Learners*, 1990, Pilgrims/Longman

MI Bill of Rights

A Student's MI Bill of Wants and Rights

Section 1

Give me time to think.
I feel I should daydream.
I shouldn't have to do eternal pair-work.
I have the right to have my own space.
Give me corrections, yes – but it's best to do this when I ask for them.
It's fine for me to look abstracted and far-away.
When you ask us for feedback, I feel like I'm at the dentist's.

_____

_____

_____

_____

I guess I'm going to mostly learn in my way, rather than in your way or anybody else's.

Section 2

Students should be permitted to talk to their neighbours during tests.
I have a right to get other people to help me with my homework.
I love activities where there is a buzz of talk.
I have a right to speak my mother tongue when I feel the need.
We have a right to demand that you are nice to us.

_____

_____

_____

_____

This is a language class, and we have a right to spend most of the time with each other, not focused on you.

© Helbling Languages 2005. Please photocopy this page for use in class.

Section 3

Give me only *real*, watertight rules.

Explain words clearly and directly – give mother-tongue translations.

Don't try and invent logic in areas of language where there is none – be up-front about this.

Give me the chance to formulate hypotheses and then check them out.

Be precise about exactly what we need in order to get ready for a test.

Tell us, in advance, how many marks different parts of the test are worth.

Explain why you have given me a particular mark.

_____

_____

_____

_____

Give me clear tables of information rather than stories and guided fantasies.

Section 4

Don't keep me nailed to a chair for 50 minutes. I have a need to stand and walk and move sometimes.

I should have the option to move or do something when I am learning.

Please involve me in action.

I have a right to role-play and move around the room.

Don't just talk and talk and talk, and write and write and write on the board.

_____

_____

_____

_____

Section 5

I want to find tunes for parts of each unit.

I have a right to use my Walkman in the reading and writing parts of lessons.

Can we have more jazz chants?

I want to sing the grammar.

I have a right to listen to music that relaxes me.

I have a right to listen to music that expresses my moods.

_____

_____

_____

_____

I have a right to music to lighten my language work.

© Helbling Languages 2005. Please photocopy this page for use in class.

Section 6
I need to know where things are.
I like exercises where I can place things in an intelligent way.
I have a right to see this grammar stuff in diagrammatic form.
I can't learn from just listening

_____

_____

_____

_____

Language is patterns. I need to see and follow them clearly.

Section 7
I have a right to enjoy the sounds of English.
Let me play with English.
Can't we do different accents in English?
I have a right to love some parts of grammar and hate others.
I have a right to let my unconscious learn English for me.
If I like some of my mistakes, then that's the way it is.

_____

_____

_____

_____

I have a right to be thrilled by the differences between English and my
mother tongue.

© Helbling Languages 2005. Please photocopy this page for use in class.

Remembering objects

Language focus	Vocabulary, speaking
Proposed MI focus	Spatial intelligence
Level	Intermediate
Time	15–25 minutes
Preparation	None.

in class

1 Tell the students to work individually and write down the name of ten objects they have seen recently (perhaps on their way to school this morning), and explain that you will help them with any they can't name in English.

2 Now ask each student to jot down when they last saw each object and when they first saw it.

3 Finally ask each student to get a clear, vivid visualisation of each object.

Group the students in fours and ask each student to explain to the others in the group exactly how they visualised the objects, and the time when they first saw each object, and when they last saw each object.

Acknowledgement
We learnt this exercise from A. R. Orage's book *On Love and Psychological Exercises*.

The exercise comes from the Gurdjieff tradition.

14 Get to know the group via MI

Language focus Diagnostic – in this exercise you will get to know a lot about the new students' breadth and depth in English. You may be listening for errors or for avoidance tactics, but most of all for the way the students feel in their English-language clothes.

Proposed MI focus All

Level Intermediate to advanced

Time Lesson 1: 20 minutes
Lesson 2: 20 minutes
Lesson 3: 20 minutes

Preparation Provide one A3 sheet of paper for each student.
Photocopy one map of Europe (page 52) per three students

in class

Lesson 1

1 Greet the students and then shut your eyes and go into a very short monologue about what you like or dislike about the area in which you live.

Now ask them to write half a page about the area in which they live. Ask them to do this in English, and tell them that they will have a choice as to whether they want to show it to anyone else in the group. (See Step 4 on page 50.)

2 Now ask each of them to take a piece of your paper and to draw the streets in the neighbourhood around the previous house/flat they lived in. (If they have always lived in the same place, then draw the streets around it.)

Group the students into fours and ask them to tell their classmates the differences between the old neighbourhood and the current one.

Listen in to the groups, so you gain some idea of each person's weaknesses and strengths in English.

3 Ask each student to think of two people in their family who they would like the other learners to meet.

The whole group sits in a big circle and the first student shows the whole group how their first person sits and how they walk. The student then shows the sitting and walking of the second person they have chosen. In both cases, they say what relationship they have with the person.

Lesson 2

1 Pair the students, and ask Person A to ask the same question over and over again (10 to 20 times):

How does music fit into your life?

Person B has to give as many different answers as he or she can.

Person B then becomes the questioner, with this repeated sentence:

What is music for you?

2 Dictate the following verses and ask the students to fill in the last two words in each:

If they made diving boards
six inches shorter
Think how much sooner
you'd be in…

To make a name for learning
when other roads are barred
Take something very easy
and make it…

TIMING TOAST
There's an art of knowing when.
Never try to guess.
Toast until it smokes and then
Twenty…

3 Ask different students to read out their endings.
(Solution: the endings are:… the water… very hard… seconds less.)

Acknowledgement

This exercise comes from Piet Hein's *Grooks II*, 1992, Blackwell's and Borgens Forlag.

Lesson 3

1 Now you need the political map of Europe; group the students in threes and give them their map. Set the students this problem:

A map publisher wants to save on the cost of using many different colours to differentiate the countries of Europe.

What is the minimum number of colours they can get away with without any adjacent countries being the same colour? (A country touching another at one point, but with no length of common border, is **not** regarded as "adjacent".)

Ask the groups to tell you about how they went about solving the problem. Explore their methodology.

2 Ask the students to introspect and to think of any time they have felt very much in tune with nature or the weather over the past few months. This can happen when walking in the mountains, or sailing, or gardening. Ask each person to briefly tell the group about any experience of this sort they have had.

(This plenary activity will give you an idea of some of the students' language strengths and weaknesses – how does each person in the group feel about expressing themselves in English?)

3 We suggest you do this exercise with classes where people already know each other. Ask all the students to put up large name panels in front of them. Ask each person to pick a person in the group they want to briefly "become". They should try and imagine what it is like to be this person, to wear this person's clothes etc. Each student then writes a one-page letter, as from this chosen person to someone else in the group.

Example:
Herbert decides to step into the shoes of Noriko, and then writes a one-page letter to Mario of the sort he guesses Noriko would write.

When each student has written his/her role-play letter, they give it to the person they have role-played. This person reads it and then gives to the addressee.

Example:
Herbert gives the letter he has written to Noriko. She reads it and gives to Mario.

At this stage the students are up and milling round the room, reading, laughing and talking.

4 Remind the learners of the half-page they wrote about their home neighbourhood in the first lesson. Ask them to re-read this, and then, if they want to, show what they have written to one or two other students.

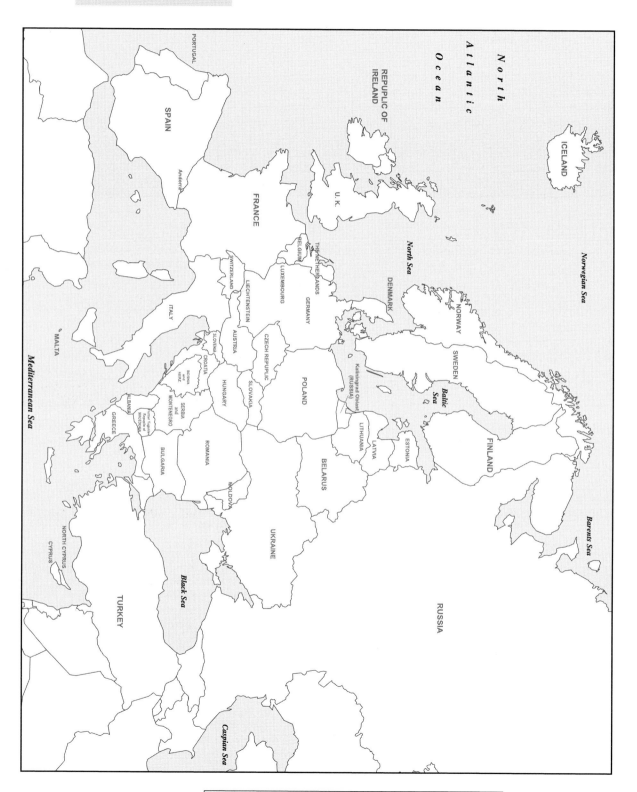

© Helbling Languages 2005. Please photocopy this page for use in class.

How many dollars?

Language focus	Listening comprehension and spelling
Proposed MI focus	Spatial and logical–mathematical
Level	Elementary to lower intermediate
Time	Lesson 1: 10–15 minutes Lesson 2: 5–10 minutes
Preparation	None.

in class

Lesson 1

1 Dictate this story to the students:

The father asked his daughter to go and buy him some things for a trip.
On his desk was an envelope with cash in it.
The girl came up to his desk and on the envelope she read 98.
She took the money and went to a shop.
There she chose 90 dollars' worth of stuff.
When she got to the cash desk she was 4 dollars short.
What had happened?

2 For homework ask the students to try and figure out what had happened. Tell them it may help if they draw a picture of the scene in the father's room. Suggest they ask for help from family and friends.

Lesson 2

1 Listen to all the solutions the students come up with, and ask them about their thinking processes. They may come up with many ingenious solutions beyond the simple spatial one, which is:

What the father, from one side of the table, had written as 86, the daughter, from her side of the table, read as 98!

Note
Although the neatest solution to this problem may be this spatial one, your students may well work interpersonally and logically–mathematically, and come up with other, marvellous solutions.

16 A logical–mathematical look at a painting

Language focus	Description
Proposed MI focus	Spatial and logical–mathematical
Level	Intermediate to advanced
Time	20–30 minutes
Preparation	Select a slide of a powerful classical painting, but ensure that its subject lies within your learners' acceptance range.
	Make one copy of the questionnaire (below) per student.

in class

1 Darken the room and show the slide of the painting. Let the students look at it for 2 to 3 minutes.

2 Read the questions, at normal speed, and ask the students to focus on two questions they really feel like answering. Say that during your second reading they should jot down those two questions, then read the questions a second time.

3 Group the students in fours to discuss the answers to the questions they have chosen.

4 Give each student the whole questionnaire, and ask them to add, individually, three more questions of their own.

5 In fours again, they work on the questions they have come up with.

Logical Quantitative Questionnaire
- What colour do you see most of in this work of art?
- What colour do you see least of in this work of art?
- Which object or shape did you see first in the painting?
- Why do you think this is the first thing you noticed?
- Look at what is happening on the canvas. Are things moving quickly or slowly?
- How can you tell?
- Make an argument for why this painting is true to life or not true to life
- Is there a hidden idea or emotion in the painting? What clues helped you find it?
- What questions might you ask the artist, to find out how he created the painting?
- What is the value of this canvas?
- How did you calculate it?

Acknowledgement
We got this questionnaire from Iole Vitti of Peanuts School, Pocos de Caldas, Brasil, and she came across it while working at Project Zero in Harvard, USA.

© Helbling Languages 2005. Please photocopy this page for use in class.

17 Prototype exercise

Language focus	Vocabulary related to space
Proposed MI focus	Logical–mathematical and spatial
Level	Intermediate to advanced
Time	20–30 minutes
Preparation	Take to class a box and an object small enough to fit into it.

in class

1 You can either hand out to each student a photocopy of the design (page 57) or put this design up on the board and ask the students to copy it.

2 Silently place the small object **in** the box and elicit: *It's in the box.*
Silently place the object **behind** the box.
Silently place the object **under** the box.
Silently place the object **next to** the box etc, each time eliciting the corresponding preposition.

3 Tell the students you want them to take a word dictation, and if they think the word you have dictated is strongly descriptive of space they should put it in one of the inner circles.

If they think it is only weakly connected to ideas about space, they should write it in one of the outer circles.
For example **IN** clearly has a strong spatial meaning, while **TO PAINT**, though involving space, is not primarily a spatial word, so TO PAINT would go in a middle or outer circle.
Dictate these words:

INSIDE	TO GO	ANTI-CLOCKWISE	ON	THROUGH
DOWNHILL	TO LIVE	ARCHITECT	NOWHERE	BRIDGE
LONDON UNDERGROUND		IN THE MOUNTAINS		
ASTRIDE	TO ARRIVE	TO BE LOCATED IN	SUNSET	PAST
REALLY	EDGE	BEYOND	SQUARE METRE	REMOTE
DOWNSTREAM		TO EXPAND	AS LONG AS	

4 Ask the students to work in threes and compare their placings of the words in terms of how spatial they feel them to be.

5 Lead a general class discussion and introduce the idea that some words belong more strongly to their class than others. Take the category FISH. Which is more "fishy", an EEL, a LOBSTER or a COD?

Prototype exercise

Variation 1

You can do this "prototype theory" exercise with many different categories of words: here are some sets you could use:

1 **Birds:** EAGLE - SEA-GULL - OWL - SPARROW - DUCK - OSTRICH - PENGUIN - HUMMING-BIRD - PEACOCK - SWAN - SWALLOW - PHEASANT - RAVEN - WREN - CHAFFINCH - KINGFISHER - CUCKOO - SKY-LARK - VULTURE - DODO - etc.

2 **Man**: MALE NURSE - POLICEMAN - DOCTOR - SOLDIER - PILOT - GENERAL - MALE MIDWIFE - COMPUTER PROGRAMMER - ENTREPRENEUR - PROFESSOR - FOOTBALLER - POLITICIAN - BOXER - HUNTER - RIDER - TEACHER - PRIEST - FARMER - DICTATOR - etc.

3 **Clothing**: HAT - BRA - DIAMOND RING - TROUSERS - STOCKINGS - SHIRT - BLOUSE - EARRINGS - JEANS - KILT - DINNER JACKET - SARI - TURBAN - SOCKS - SWIMMING CAP - HANDBAG - GLASSES - PULLOVER - OVERCOAT - UNDERPANTS - SCARF - etc.

Variation 2

Propose the idea of SMELL, and set half the class the task, as their homework, of getting together a set of 20 words that are more or less in the area of smell.

Give them the first three:
• bread
• lavender
• steam.

The other half of the class work on TASTE:
• sardines
• egg shells
• tomato sauce.

In the next lesson, the SMELL people pair off with the TASTE people and dictate their words to their partners, as in the activity above.

Acknowledgement

We would probably not have come up with Variation 2 without the ideas we found in Sheelagh Deller's *Lessons from the Learner*, 1992, Pilgrims-Longman.

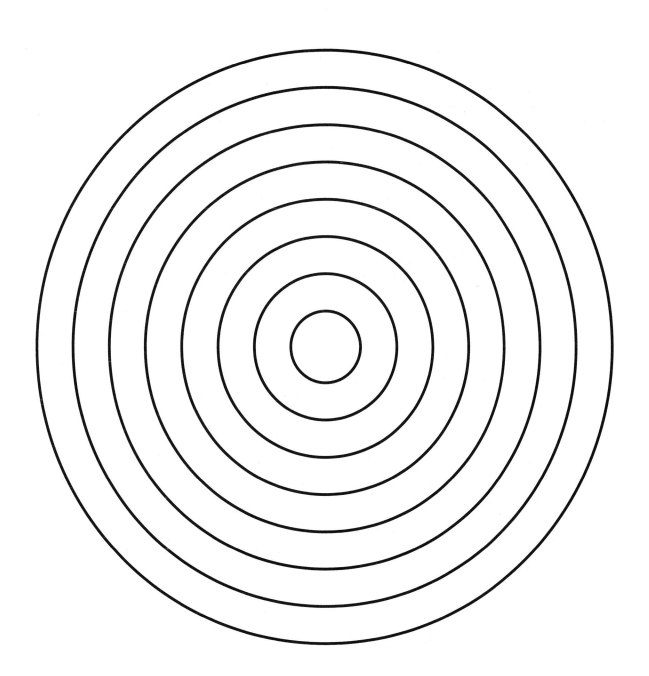

© Helbling Languages 2005. Please photocopy this page for use in class.

18

Which are X's strong intelligences?

Language focus	Speaking
Proposed MI focus	All
Level	Elementary to advanced (but do this unit only when your students are already reasonably familiar with MI thinking)
Time	20–30 minutes
Preparation	None.

in class

1 Ask the students each to turn a sheet of paper around so it's landscape, and draw a line across it, near the top, like this:

Music intelligence

strong --weak

Ask them to draw another six similar lines down the page for the other intelligences.

2 Ask each student to bring to mind someone they know well.

Tell them to think about how strong this person is in each of the intelligences, and mark the place between strong and weak along the relevant line.

If they feel this person is strong in, say, musical things, ask them to think of how their person shows this.

3 Get the students to work in threes, telling each other about their three people and the strengths they feel they have in the different areas.

Examples:

Spatial

strong_____X_____weak

Mario, thinking about his own father, Giuseppe, thinks he was pretty strong spatially. When designing a church, Giuseppe would typically sketch the idea for the building onto a scrap of paper. He would then water-colour the church into its landscape. The mathematics of the design came much later.

Linguistic

strong_____X_____weak

Mario thinks Giuseppe was less strong in his language intelligence. He spoke English, his adopted language, with a strong Italian accent. His cultural expression stayed unbendingly Italian after 40 years in the UK. But he had a large and powerful English vocabulary. In his mother tongue he was much more interested in ideas than in style or language form, etc.

Which intelligences do we use in reading?

Language focus   The nature of the reading process

Proposed MI focus   All

Level   Elementary to advanced
(In the case of the reading given here, upper intermediate)

Time   20–30 minutes

Preparation   Copy the reading passage (page 60) so each student can have one.
Prepare to read the passage aloud to the class.

in class

1 Ask the students to read the passage to themselves.

Ask them to write two paragraphs about what went through their heads as they were reading.

2 Read the passage aloud to them.

3 Now give them time and space to tell you in detail about their process during their first silent read, and then as they listened. For example:

- were they in a spatial mode or in a musical mode?
- did they feel right in the action themselves?
- or were they well outside, thinking about the style of the writing?
- or were they in a daydream unconnected with the text?

Listen to their process stories with uncritical openness. Your receptivity will help their stories flow.

When you hear the untrammelled reality of the reading and listening processes, it's breath-taking!

Reading Passage

"What time is it?" he asks.

"Three o'clock."

"Morning or afternoon?"

"Afternoon."

He is silent. There is nothing else he wants to know. Only that another block
of time has passed.

"How are you?" I say.

"Who is it?" he asks.

"It's the doctor. How do you feel?"

He does not answer right away.

"Feel?" he says.

"I hope you feel better," I say.

I press the button at the side of the bed.

"Down you go," I say.

"Yes, down," he says.

He falls back upon the bed awkwardly. His stumps, unweighed by legs and
feet, rise in the air, presenting themselves. I unwrap the bandages from the
stumps and begin to cut away the black scabs and dead, glazed fat with
scissors and forceps. A shard of white bone comes loose. I pick it away.

I wash the wounds with disinfectant and re-dress the stumps.

All this while he does not speak.

What is he thinking behind those eyes that do not blink?

"Anything more I can do for you?" I ask.

For a long moment he is silent.

"Yes," he says at last and without the least irony, "you can bring me a pair
of shoes."

(From *Confessions of a Knife*, Richard Selzer, 1982, Triad/Granada, page 134)

© Helbling Languages 2005. Please photocopy this page for use in class.

20 Fun with maths

Language focus	Listening and carrying out precise mathematical instructions
Proposed MI focus	Mathematical
Level	Lower intermediate upwards
Time	10 minutes
Preparation	None.

in class

1 Announce that you can read the minds of a high percentage of students in class. On a sheet of paper, write "a grey elephant in Denmark", fold the paper so that nobody can read what you have written, give the folded paper to a student and ask him or her to keep it until the end of the activity, without reading it.

2 Write the alphabet across the board, and put the corresponding number below each letter, e.g. 1 under A, 4 under D etc.

3 Ask your students to have pen and paper ready, and give them the following instructions (making sure they have all completed their calculations before you move on):

a) think of a number from 2 to 9
b) multiply the number by 9
c) add the two digits together
d) subtract 5
e) check on the board to convert the answer into a letter of the alphabet
f) write down the name of a European country beginning with that letter
g) write down a four-legged animal beginning with the second letter of that country
h) write down a typical colour for that animal.

4 Ask the student with the folded paper to unfold it and read out to the class what you wrote at the beginning of the exercise.

Note
If you have a few maths whizz-kids in your class, they might like to try working out the logic behind this activity, possibly in co-operation with their maths teacher.

Acknowledgement
We learnt about this activity from Ken Wilson, the Director of the English Speaking Theatre, at the IATEFL Conference in Katowice, Poland, in November 1999.

CHAPTER 2
TEACHING FROM YOUR COURSEBOOK

From hand to voice

21

Language focus	Internalizing grammar structures
Proposed MI focus	Linguistic, spatial and kinaesthetic
Level	Lower intermediate to advanced
Time	30–40 minutes
Preparation	Find a couple of paragraphs that carry the main new grammar points. Get five people with very different handwriting each to copy them out on a single sheet of paper.
	Photocopy the sheet, one per student.

in class

1 Group the students in fours and give each foursome two sheets of handwritten paragraphs.

2 Dictate the following questionnaire to them:
   - How does each person write their letter "h"?
   - Do the letters slope to the left or to the right?
   - Where is the dot over the letter "i"?
   - Does this writer press heavily, or is their hand a light one?
   - How many letters does the writer join up?
   - Is this person a fast or slow writer?
   - Is this a male or female hand?

3 Ask the students to answer the above questions about each of the five texts.

4 Now ask the foursomes to choose the handwriting that they find most interesting.

5 Ask them to rehearse reading the text aloud as they guess the owner of that handwriting would.

6 Each group reads the passage aloud to the rest. The task of the listeners is to decide on the gender and age of the person who wrote the text.

Note
By the time they have finished this exercise they will know the textbook paragraphs virtually by heart. The graphological and voice tasks usefully mask the underlying language aim: internalisation of the language patterns presented.

Acknowledgement
Simon Marshall, author of *From Advanced Speaker to Native*, got us interested in handwriting, and *Cours Pratique de Graphologie*, by André Lecerf, 1976, Editions Dangles, has proved an invaluable background book.

Changing handwriting

Language focus	Listening and internalizing vocabulary and grammar.
Proposed MI focus	Interpersonal, linguistic, spatial, kinaesthetic
Level	Post-beginner to advanced
Time	20–30 minutes
Preparation	Choose a passage to dictate. This could usefully be a text from your coursebook two or three units beyond the place you have reached with this class. Prepare to dictate the first third of the text in a whisper, and the next third in a slow, warm voice. Prepare to read the last part in a normal speaking voice .

in class

1 Tell the class they are going to take down a dictation.

Whisper the first part of the passage, or play the cassette.

Speak the next bit in a slow, warm voice.

Speak the last part normally.

2 Ask the students to swap their dictation with a partner. Each person copies out the first ten words their partner wrote while listening to first the whisper, then the slow voice and finally the normal speaking voice

Ask each person to imitate their partner's handwriting as accurately as they can, getting the same space between words, the same breaks within words, the same slant to the letters and the same letter shaping as their partner.

3 Ask the partners to come together and share what they have noticed.

4 Allow whole class time for general feedback on the exercise, which is amazing when you experience it for the first time.

Intensive reading

Language focus   The meaning of separate sentences, contrasted with the meaning of the passage from which they come. Assimilation of new grammar and vocabulary from the coursebook.

Proposed MI focus   Logical–mathematical

Level   Post-beginner to advanced

Time   20–30 minutes

Preparation   Choose six to eight sentences from the next passage in the coursebook.

in class

1 Tell the students you will be dictating some sentences, and that they should leave gaps down the page between the sentences. Then dictate the six to eight sentences in random order, and not in the order they occur in the coursebook passage.

Allow the students time to ask vocabulary and comprehension questions.

2 Ask the students to fold and tear the page they have been writing on into slips, with a separate sentence on each slip.

Tell them to work individually or in pairs, and to arrange the sentences into categories. There must be more than one category, and there must be fewer categories than the total number of sentences. Their categories can be of any sort: semantic, emotional, grammatical, arithmetical (e.g. six-word sentences) or anything else that occurs to them. Try not to give them more than one example of what you mean by "category", because examples hem them in. In a post-beginner class, your explanations will be in the mother tongue.

Tell them to give each category a written heading. In a low-level class you will need to give plenty of help with vocabulary.

3 Ask different people around the room to give you their headings, which you put on the board, and then ask them to read out the sentences under those headings. If the class is post-beginner, there will be natural recourse to mother tongue in explaining the categories.

4 Now ask the class to read the passage in the coursebook from which the sentences were taken. Allow time for students to comment on the whole exercise.

Acknowledgement
This way of thinking stems directly from Dr Caleb Gattegno's mathematical approach to language teaching.

24 Making sentences vanish

Language focus	Asking questions
Proposed MI focus	Linguistic and logical–mathematical Variation 2 appeals to the spatial intelligence
Level	Lower intermediate to intermediate
Time	10 minutes
Preparation	Prepare a long sentence or a paragraph as a basis for the text-deleting game.

in class

1 Write a long sentence or a paragraph on the board or dictate it to a student who writes it on the board.

Example:

Students frequently have no say in choosing the kinds of texts that their teachers decide they have to study or write in their exercise books; maybe this is why a considerable number of students gain a lot of pleasure when given the opportunity to erase parts of a text or a complete text dictated by a teacher, which is what this activity is all about.

2 Tell the students to ask you specific questions about the text. Whenever a word or a chunk of language in the text is the direct answer to a question they have asked, you erase this bit from the text. So if a student for example says, *Who often has no say in choosing text?* you erase the word *Students*. Another student may then come up with *What is the opposite of 'seldom'?* and you rub out *frequently*. Etc.....

3 When a question is linguistically incorrect, shrug your shoulders and in this way give the question back to the class to correct. *Rub out the word only when the question has been asked correctly.*

4 You will notice that when isolated function words, such as *why*, are left, students will start asking meta-grammatical questions, such as *When you ask the reason for something, what's the first word in your question?*

Variation 1

You can turn this activity into one that is yet more logically–mathematically focused by awarding points for the number of words deleted in one go.

For example, the question *What happens frequently?* would knock out all the 23 words from *have no say* to *exercise books*, so the student asking this question would then get 23 points.

The variation proposed here is psychologically very different from the main exercise, as it introduces competition where before there had been a collaborative effort.

Variation 2

Ask a student who is good at drawing to come to the board and produce a really cluttered picture with far too many things in it. This can best be done by a student who has already finished an activity that the rest of the class is still working on.

Tell the class the picture needs visually emptying to become visually satisfying. They get rid of the clutter by asking questions that "empty" the picture. The artist deletes. It is his/her decision when the picture has become sparse enough.

Acknowledgement

We got this idea from a Pilgrims colleague, Judy Baker, and the exercise family to which this activity belongs would not exist without the work of Caleb Gattegno.

For more logical–mathematical and linguistic activities of this sort see Section 2 of *Grammar Games*, Rinvolucri, 1984, CUP, and Section 2 of *More Grammar Games,* Davis and Rinvolucri, 1995, CUP.

Retrospective prediction

Language focus Revision of grammar and vocabulary in a previous unit

Proposed MI focus Linguistic (highly auditory) and interpersonal

Level Post-beginner to upper intermediate

Time 10–15 minutes

Preparation Choose the unit of the coursebook you want the students to revise.

in class

1 Get the class standing or sitting in a circle.

2 Ask for a volunteer reader, and tell that person to open the coursebook at the page on which they will find the reading passage you have selected. Everybody else has their books closed.

Tell the reader to read the first sentence, and then the first word of the second sentence. Then they should pause, and the student to their left has to guess the next word.

If the guess is wrong, the reader reads the first and second words of the sentence, and the next student round to the left has to try and guess word three.

When a student guesses correctly, the current reader continues reading through to the end of the sentence, then the correct guesser takes the open book and becomes the reader. They read the next sentence in full, and stop at a point of their choice in the following sentence for the person on their left to guess the next word. And so on round the circle.

Variation
Instead of stopping short for the student on the reader's left to supply the next word, get the reader to read to change one word in each sentence they read.

The task of the person to their left is to pick out the "wrong" word and to suggest the correct one.

Acknowledgement
Robert O'Neill offered the teachers who used his *Kernels Intermediate* in the early 1970s the use of the technique above and its variation. What we have proposed is that the students should do all the work and reap all the language benefits, while teachers are left free of any performance role, giving time and space for observation of, and thought about, their students.

Disguising voices

Language focus	Preview of the grammar and vocabulary of a unit that is two further on in the coursebook than the unit your students have reached
Proposed MI focus	Linguistic (highly auditory) and interpersonal
Level	Lower intermediate to intermediate
Time	Lesson 1: 5 minutes Lesson 2: 15–20 minutes
Preparation	For lesson 2, a tape player

in class

Lesson 1

Having counted the number of paragraphs in your chosen coursebook passage, assign each paragraph to a separate student. If there are seven paragraphs then seven students will be involved.

For homework, tell each one to record their paragraph onto an audio cassette. *Tell them to disguise their voices* so that no one in the class will recognise their recording. Suggest they imitate the voice of a pop singer they know well, or someone in their own family – or maybe they could imitate a young child or an alien.

Lesson 2

1 Collect the students' recordings.

2 Play the first recording and stop it the moment anybody in the class can correctly identify the speaker.

3 Move quickly to the second recording, etc.

Variation

In contexts where the majority of students do not have access to cassette recorders at home, the exercise could be done in class with students, with their eyes closed, listening to their colleagues reading aloud from the textbook.

Alternatively, if students don't have access to tape-recorders, the school could make one available for students to record with.

Note

In this activity the focus is strongly interpersonal and auditory, but when, two weeks later, you come to study the unit in question, the students will shoot through the reading text with fresh memories of the game. This is because the reading text will have been to some extent personalised.

Acknowledgement

We have adapted this unit from 'Mystery Voices', page 45 in *Games for Thinking*, by Robert Fisher, 1997, Nash Pollock Publishing,

Speed up!

Language focus	Internalisation of part of a coursebook reading passage.
Proposed MI focus	Kinaesthetic and linguistic
Level	Beginner to advanced
Time	5–10 minutes
Preparation	Get a chocolate bar. N.B. This exercise is ideal if you are suddenly asked to take another teacher's class.

in class

1 Choose a coursebook passage two units ahead. Tell the students that the person who manages to copy the most words in this passage correctly in 120 seconds will win the chocolate bar.

2 With their pens at the ready give them:

Ready, steady, GO!

3 At the end of 120 seconds, ask the students to mark each other's work, and then to count the number of correct words. Award the chocolate bar to the person with the highest score.

Note
After this brief activity, students will be well on the way to becoming acquainted with some of the language content of the unit two ahead.

Guess my sentence

Language focus	Vocabulary revision, sentence grammar, sentence stress
Proposed MI focus	Musical-rhythmical, verbal-linguistic
Level	Lower intermediate to advanced
Time	5–10 minutes
Preparation	None.

in class

1 Ask students to think of a text you have recently worked on with them. Get them to call out words they remember from the text. Write the words on the board.

2 Point to a word. Tell the students that you are going to create a sentence with this word, and ask them to work in pairs and guess the sentence. Do not tell them the sentence, but instead, clap the rhythm of the sentence or tap it out on a tambourine. Repeat the rhythm as often as they want.

3 Ask the class to call out their suggestions. When a sentence comes close to your original one, get the student who has called it out to repeat it. Signal nonverbally that it is not quite the sentence you had in mind, and encourage the whole class to make more suggestions. Use mime and gesture only to elicit the original sentence from the class.

4 Carry on like this with another word from the board.

Variation
After some time, you could ask a student to take over your role.

Acknowledgement
The idea of getting students to guess a chunk of language from a rhythm beaten on a tambourine comes from Glen Stephen.

The Roman room

Language focus	Language of furniture and room design
Proposed MI focus	Visual-spatial
Level	Lower intermediate upwards
Time	Lesson 1: 30 minutes Lesson 2: 20 minutes
Preparation	None.

in class

Lesson 1

1 Ask your students to work on their own and imagine the room of their dreams. Get them to think about the shape and size of the room, where they would like windows and doors, what pieces of furniture, and what colours they would like to have in that room. Tell them they are free to be creative – e.g. if they want a river to flow through their room, there it is. However, the room should be clearly structured and without too many details so that they can easily remember it.

2 Tell them to draw a floor plan of the room.

3 Put them into pairs and ask them to describe their rooms to each other, using the ground plans they have created.

4 Ask them each to write a list of 20 objects. This list should have no connection with the room they have been describing. Tell them to swap their lists and memorize the 20 objects in the order in which they occur in the list. Give them three minutes to do this.

5 In pairs, they check how many of the objects each student remembers of her own list. Tell them they should check how many objects from the list their partner remembers.

6 Compare the outcomes by asking how many objects the students have remembered. Ask the students how they went about memorising the lists.

7 As an assignment for the next lesson, ask them to internalise as many details as possible of the room they have created. They should be able to remember their room well without looking at the floor plan. (You will need to give them an explanation for this homework, because otherwise some students may find it very strange and might not do it; tell them that you are going to teach them a powerful memory strategy, for which a precondition is that they will have internalised their ground plans.)

Lesson 2

1 In the next class, pair them up with different partners and ask them each to write another list of 20 objects.

2 Tell them to swap the lists. They should imagine that they are in their room now, walking round the room once in a circular movement, starting at a certain point and coming back to the same point in the end. It is up to them whether they want to 'walk' clockwise or anti-clockwise. They place one object after the other from the list on pieces of furniture, the floor, window sills etc. Ask them to create strong images as they are doing so, for example by distorting the size relationships and making their objects disproportionately larger or smaller, adding sounds and smells etc. Allow three minutes for this.

3 In pairs, the students again check how well each of them remembers their room this time round.

4 Ask if this exercise could be of use to them in studying information they need to remember.

Variation

The "room" technique is especially good for helping students remember abstract words. Where in the room would you put words like *hope, gap, telepathy?*

Precisely because the placing is not obvious, the student makes a greater effort and so the memory effect is stronger.

Note

Placing words from the coursebook in an imaginary room is an extremely effective way of mobilising the memory.

Acknowledgement

We found this technique in Tony Buzan's book *Use Your Memory*, BBC Publications, first published in 1986. Buzan comments that this mnemonic technique was invented more than 2000 years ago by the Romans, hence its name.

Making a coursebook dialogue physical or musical

Language focus   Intensive listening and reading

Proposed MI focus   Kinaesthetic and musical

Level   Post-beginner to advanced

Time   40–50 minutes

Preparation   You'll need the tape-recording of your chosen coursebook dialogue, and a tape player.

Ask one of your students who likes drama to choose a scene or dialogue from a previous unit in the coursebook, and to prepare a mime based on it. Also ask two or three musically talented students to pick a previous dialogue, and prepare to present it musically, using voice and maybe instruments.

in class

1 Ask your mime artist to perform. All the students silently re-read the dialogue/scene from the book. The mime is repeated.

Then ask the musicians to present their dialogue/scene.

2 Ask the students to listen carefully to the new coursebook dialogue, books closed. Deal with language difficulties, and then play the dialogue a second time.

3 Tell the students to open their books and read the new dialogue. Ask each of the students to choose whether they prefer to re-present it in mime or as a song.

4 Divide the class into two groups: the mimers and the singers. Let these groups sub-divide into numbers that correspond to the number of roles in the dialogue. Give them 15 minutes for preparation time.

5 Give each group of singers and mimers a chance to perform to the whole class.

Note
After this apparently game-like activity, the students will have the new grammar presented by the dialogue firmly somewhere down there in their linguistic sub-consciousness.

Storyboarding
the coursebook dialogue

Language focus	Intensive listening and intensive reading
Proposed MI focus	Interpersonal and spatial
Level	Post-beginner to intermediate
Time	40–50 minutes
Preparation	Choose a dialogue from a future unit in your coursebook. Photocopy the text without any picture material round it.

in class

1 Play the tape with the dialogue once, then help the students with unknown words or chunks.

2 Ask the students to visualise WHERE the dialogue is taking place. They listen again and shout out their ideas.

3 Before the students listen a third time, ask them to decide how the people are dressed and what they look like.

4 Give out the photocopied dialogue and let them read it. They may have further questions about meaning.

5 Draw an empty six-frame storyboard so they can all see it. Explain that they are to work in pairs as if they were going to film the dialogue. Get them to select six moments in the dialogue, and in each of the six frames they draw what the camera will see; underneath each picture they write in the corresponding text. Give them 15 minutes for this work.

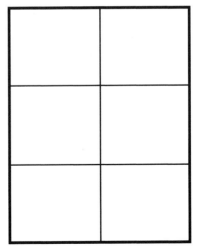

6 They stick their frames up on the walls and go round to see the films that the others have imagined.

Variation
This is an excellent way of getting upper-intermediate and advanced students to read deep into a short literary passage.

A game of parts

Language focus	Learning word shape and guessing from meaning. The passage given here teaches weather words
Proposed MI focus	Logical–mathematical and spatial
Level	Beginner to intermediate, according to the difficulty of the text used. The passage here is for intermediate level
Time	15–20 minutes
Preparation	Choose a short text and decide which syllables and letters you are going to blank out. You could put this on an OHP transparency or use the board. You could use the text given below for intermediate level.

This technique can be used with part of the reading passage in the coursebook unit you are currently doing. You can also use it for previewing units ahead or revising units already covered. |

in class

1 Pre-teach any words the students may not know.

2 Put up your transparency or write up the text you have chosen on the board with the gaps you have decided on:

Things that f____ from the sky

Snow. Hail. I do not ____ke sleet, but when it is mi____ with pure ____ite snow it is very __tty. Snow looks won____ when it has ____llen on a roof of cypress bark.
When snow ____ins to melt a ____tle, or when ____ly a small am____ has fallen, it ____ters into all the cracks ____ween the tiles, so that the r_____ is black in some places, pure ____ite in others – most attra_____.
I like drizz____ and hail ____en they come ____wn on a shingle roof.
I also like ____ost on a shingle roof or in a ____rden.

3 Ask students to come up freely and add in the syllables and letters they reckon are missing.

4 Help the class with any gaps they have not yet filled.

Variation
Ask a student to choose a song or other text they like, and come to class with a gapped version to put up on the board or OHP. The exercise is done the same way, but the power of text choice is in student hands.

Acknowledgement
Guessing covered parts of a word in a poem was a pastime among court ladies in 10th-century Japan. The game is mentioned in *The Pillow Book of Sei Shonagon* (1967, Penguin), and the text above is taken from page 210 of the same book.

Musical, spatial or kinaesthetic?

Language focus	Vocabulary revision, irregular verbs
Proposed MI focus	Musical, spatial and kinaesthetic
Level	Lower intermediate to advanced
Time	20–30 minutes
Preparation	Go through the vocabulary of the previous three to five units and pick out words that, in your mind, could belong in the area of the musical, the kinaesthetic or the spatial intelligences. Pick out 20 to 30 words.

Alternatively you could use the words below.

in class

1 Tell each student to make four columns on a new sheet of paper.
Tell them to give the columns these headings:

Music   **Space**   **Movement**   **None of these**

Explain that you are going to dictate some words to them. They should quickly decide whether this word has to do with music or any of the other three categories, and write it under the correct heading.
A word may go in two categories.

2 Dictate the words you have selected, or the words given here:

SING   RUN   CHURCH   OCEAN   CANARY

POTATO   MEMORY   TO DANCE   OVER THERE

STRAIGHT ON   PIANO   HORSE   BUS DRIVER

JANUARY   COMFORTABLE   SHRILL   THINKING

DRIVING   JUDO   DEEP   FAR AWAY   REPETITION

TO THROW   TO SHOUT   FOG

3 Group the learners in threes, and ask them to compare their placings of the words. Ask them to concentrate on the ones that they felt sure of.

Variation

Ask each student to draw a line across their page like this:

Things I do on my own   Things I do with /to others

Tell them you are going to dictate the infinitive of several irregular verbs, and they should select how far along the line they think the verb belongs. Then they should write all three forms of the verb, in a short list, beneath the part of the line that seems right.

Here are some verbs:

WAKE UP	BE	READ	HURT	BUY
DREAM	MEET	SING	SAY	
SWIM	PAY	HAVE	SPELL	TELL

Group the students in threes to compare their placings. Help them check the spelling and pronunciation of the parts of the verbs.

Percussion punctuation

Language focus	Reading aloud, intonation, pausing and punctuation
Proposed MI focus	Musical, kinaesthetic and linguistic
Level	Elementary to advanced
Time	20–30 minutes
Preparation	Choose a passage from a coursebook unit or any text appropriate for the students' level, and count the number of punctuation marks in the passage you have chosen.

Alternatively, use the passage, 'Looking for something' (see page 82). These are the punctuation marks in it:

" ! " . , : ?

Alternatively, use the passage, 'Looking for something' (see page 82).

in class

1 Write the punctuation marks from your chosen passage on the board. Check that the students know the English words for them.

2 Divide the class into groups. There should be as many people in each group as there are punctuation marks in the passage, plus one; if necessary, two students can share a punctuation mark.

Ask the students to look at the text chosen.

3 Explain that the student in each group who didn't get a punctuation mark is going to read the text aloud, and that the other six are each to choose one of the punctuation marks and to choose a sound and action to represent it. One student might clap once for a full stop, another might crackle a crisp-bag to represent inverted commas, and a third might cough for a comma.

Tell the students to take their time choosing sounds they like, and then ask each group to practise reading the text aloud with sounds in place of punctuation marks. The groups do this work simultaneously.

So the sentence *"Kiss me," she said!* might go like this:

Student A:	bang!
Student B (reader):	kiss me
Student C:	squeak!
Student A:	bang!
Student B (reader):	she said
Student D:	rustle!

The students need to practise the piece several times so that the reading is fluent and the people making the punctuation sound or action come in on cue.

4 Ask each group to do a sound-punctuated reading in front of the whole class.

5 Ask a whole group to decide which is the best sound for a full stop. The full-stop people from every group adopt that sound. Go round the groups, doing the same with the other five marks.

Finally ask one student to read while the whole group punctuate with the sounds they have decided they like best.

Repeat, but this time slower.

Repeat, but this time faster.

Repeat, but this time softer etc.

A possible reading text:

Looking for something

John was out in the garden, looking for something. He was on hands and knees in a flower border. His wife saw him from an upstairs window, opened the window and called down to him:

"What are you doing?"

"I'm looking for my keys."

"Your keys? Lost them in the garden, did you?" she asked.

"No, in the house."

"Then why are you looking for them in the garden?"

He straightened his back and looked up to her:

"The light's better in the garden!"

Acknowledgement

We learnt this activity from Maggie Farrer, Principal of the University of the First Age, Birmingham, UK, where all the work done is along MI lines. In 1998 the UFI offered summer courses to over 2000 middle-school kids.

CHAPTER 3
LOOKING OUT

Talking as someone else

Language focus	Asking questions, talking about oneself, focused listening, presentation skills
Proposed MI focus	Interpersonal and intrapersonal
Level	Intermediate upwards
Time	30–40 minutes (depending on the size of the class)
Preparation	None.

in class

1 Ask the students to work in pairs, preferably choosing a partner they do not yet know very well.

2 Student A starts asking questions, trying to find out as much as possible about student B. Allow 5 minutes for this.

3 Ask them to swap roles. Give another 5 minutes for student B to interview student A.

4 Ask the students to take pen and paper, and individually create a mind map or write a list of what they remember about their partner.

5 Get the students to sit in a circle. Tell them that they are going to introduce their partner to the group in the following way:

One student begins. They stand behind the student they are introducing, have their hands on the other person's shoulders, culture permitting, and talk as if they were the other person (speaking in first person singular). The student who is being introduced listens without interrupting.

Ask them to notice their own and the others' reactions to the introduction. Each person has a maximum of 2 minutes to introduce their partner.

6 Ask students how they felt during the activity, and give them opportunity to "correct" anything that was said about them or add information if they would like to.

Note
This activity works best at the beginning of a course. If you have more than 16 or so students, do steps 5 and 6 in two separate groups. We have found that the feedback to the group phase works best in groups of 8 to 16.

Variation
Should you want to use this exercise later in a course, ask the students to interview each other about a person the interviewee knows well, like, say, a relative. In the feedback session the reporting student says *I am X; who is John's uncle*, John being her classmate.

Multiple interviewers

Language focus	Listening and using interrogative forms
Proposed MI focus	Interpersonal
Level	Elementary to advanced
Time	15–20 minutes
Preparation	None.

in class

1 Ask for one student to volunteer to be interviewed about a topic of her choice, and ask for a volunteer interviewer.

2 Tell the group that any time anyone wants to take over as interviewer, they just go up and touch the current interviewer on the shoulder; they then take over as interviewer.

Students can also replace the interviewee in the same way.

A group member can do this at any time.

3 Explain that the idea is to do it in a harmonious way, so that the interview proceeds smoothly.

Acknowledgement
We learnt this exercise from Penelope Williams.

Writing a cinquain

Language focus	Creative writing
Proposed MI focus	Linguistic
Level	Lower intermediate
Time	30–40 minutes
Preparation	Write one or two sample cinquains onto an OHP transparency or poster paper (see the example below).

in class

1 Display your cinquains and read them out to your class.

Example:

My friend –
Fun, laughter, tears.
You're always there for me.
No one listens to me like you.
Partner.

2 Tell your students that a cinquain is a special poetic form that is more than 600 years old. Ask them to work with a partner and find the rules which govern the forms of a cinquain. They are as follows:

Line 1: 2 syllables; gives the subject of the poem.

Line 2: 4 syllables; describes the subject of the poem in a few words.

Line 3: 6 syllables; relates to an action or actions that have to do with the subject.

Line 4: 8 syllables; expresses the author's feeling about the subject.

Line 5: 2 syllables; names the subject again, but with a different word (or words).

3 Tell your students to write their own cinquain. You might like to set them a topic, or alternatively give them the choice to write on whatever they choose.

Acknowledgement
We learnt this technique from Hans Eberhard Piepho. Another, similar idea, where students are expected to write to a very strict form, is the writing of Mini-Sagas (short narrative texts of exactly 50 words, title not more than 15 words). See, for example, *The Book of Mini Sagas*, 1985, Alan Sutton.

What does it mean?

Language focus	Ambiguity
Proposed MI focus	Linguistic and logical–mathematical
Level	Advanced
Time	10–20 minutes
Preparation	Copy the text below, one for each student.

1 Pair the students and ask them to translate this text together; give out one copy between two. Don't breathe a word about the ambiguous nature of the text.

You write to ask me for my opinion of X, who has applied for a position in your department. I cannot recommend him too highly or say enough good things about him. There is no other student of mine with whom I can adequately compare him. His thesis is the sort of work you don't expect to see nowadays and in it he has clearly demonstrated his manifest capabilities. The amount of material he knows will surprise you. You will indeed be fortunate if you can get him to work for you.

(If you have a class with many mother tongues, pair as many of the students as is possible according to mother tongue, and let the others work on their own.)

2 Bring the pairs together in fours to compare their versions.

Ask for a show of hands from those who would be pleased to get a reference like this

Acknowledgement
We found the text above on page 43 of *A Mathematician Reads the Newspaper*, John Allen Paulos, 1995, Basic Books, Harper Collins.

© Helbling Languages 2005. Please photocopy this page for use in class.

The spin of a coin

Language focus	Making suggestions
Proposed MI focus	Logical–mathematical and kinaesthetic
Level	Intermediate to advanced
Time	30–45 minutes
Preparation	Write solution cards (see A–D below), making one card for each text. Copy enough for two cards to be given out to each group of five students. Take a handful of coins – low-value, for preference – to class.

in class

1 Pair the students and ask them to gamble for a fictitious $1000 by tossing a coin. The first student to get six "heads" will be the winner.

2 Write this text up on the board:

   John and his friend, Paul, agree that the first to get heads six times will win.

   An earth tremor interrupts the game after eight flips, with John leading by five heads to Paul's three.

   What do you think they should do about the $1000?

3 Group the students in fives. Give one solution card to each group and ask them to discuss the solution suggested and brainstorm other solutions, then write these down on a separate piece of paper.

4 Give a second solution card to each group.

5 Each group choose their favourite solution from the two cards they've now got, and read it out to the class.

6 End with a brief, whole-class, feedback session.

Texts for solution cards:

A *John gets the $1000, given that the contest was an all-or-nothing one and that he was ahead at the time when the earth tremor stopped play.*

B *They each take half the prize money, as the game turned out to be a non-contest and as this is the friendliest way of proceeding.*

C *They should split the prize money in proportion to the number of heads they got. This leaves John with 5/8ths and Paul with 3/8ths of the amount.*

D *If the game were to be re-started, Paul's only chance of winning would be to land 3 heads in a row. The probability of him doing this is 1 in 8. So John ought to pocket 7/8ths of the cash, leaving Paul with 1/8th.*

Acknowledgement
We owe this lesson plan to the French mathematician, Pascal; see page 47 of *A Mathematician Reads the Newspaper* by John Allen Paulos, Basic Books, 1995, Harper Collins.

© Helbling Languages 2005. Please photocopy this page for use in class.

Alphabet dialogues

Language focus	Dialogue-writing within a formal constraint
Proposed MI focus	Linguistic, intrapersonal and interpersonal
Level	Post-beginner to intermediate
Time	20–30 minutes
Preparation	Bring in two large sheets of paper to stick to the board.

in class

1 Ask for a volunteer to come to the board and write a dialogue with you. Tell them to write their first line of a dialogue with you on the right hand side of the board, while you write the first line of another dialogue with them on the left hand side. The first word of both your sentence and of theirs must start with the letter "A".

2 Change places and reply to each other's first line. (Tell them to reply to you while, simultaneously, you reply to them.) You must both start your replies with the letter "B".

3 Send the volunteer back to their place and pair the students. Ask each students to write on a separate sheet of paper, and follow the model above so the members of each pair write simultaneous dialogues to each other. Then, instead of changing places, the student swap the sheets of paper. The first line of each dialogue must start with the letter "C". The response must start with the letter "D" and so on. Tell them to write six utterances, so the last one will start with the letter "H".

4 Ask three or four pairs to read out both their dialogues.

Note
An arbitrary restriction like the one above will often provoke a lot of language creativity.

Variation
Another good "creative restriction" is to ask the dialogue writers to avoid declarative or negative sentences and use only questions, so that a dialogue might go like this:

A: *Are you ready to go?*

B: *What's your guess?*

A: *Shall we take the car?*

B: *What, just down to the end of the street?*

A: *D'you realise how long this street is?*

Alphabet dialogues

This technique is used in shows like *Whose Line is it Anyway?*, and in Tom Stoppard's *Rosenkrantz and Guildenstern are Dead* :

Rosenkrantz:	We could play at questions.
Guildenstern:	What good would that do?
Rosenkrantz:	Practice!
Guildenstern:	Statement! One-love.
Rosenkrantz:	Cheating!
Guildenstern:	How?
Rosenkrantz:	I hadn't started yet.
Guildenstern:	Statement. Two-love.
Rosenkrantz:	Are you counting that?

Acknowledgement

We found the main idea for this game in *Language Play* by David Crystal, 1998, Penguin.

How many questions?

Language focus	Interrogative forms
Proposed MI focus	Spatial or musical, logical–mathematical , interpersonal and linguistic.
Level	Post-beginner to intermediate
Time	30–40 minutes
Preparation	Bring to class a picture or an object large enough for everyone to see. Alternatively bring a music recording that's 3–5 minutes long.

in class

1 Brainstorm the class for all the question words and sentence starters for questions that the students know, so that you come up with a good long list which will include *when, where, how long, what, how, is there, are there*, etc. Write these on the board.

2 Pair the students and show them the chosen picture or object, or play the piece of music. Explain that they have 10 minutes to write as many questions as they can about the object/picture/music. Each questions generated by a pair must have different content.

3 Ask the pairs to count how many questions they have produced.

4 The pair with the most questions now read out their sentences slowly, so the others can challenge content repetition or language incorrectness. Any challenge you support knocks that question out.

5 The winning pair is the one with largest number of questions remaining, that have been accepted by the class and by you.

6 Ask each pair to write their two most interesting questions on the board.

7 Ask the class to pick the three they most want an answer to.

8 Ask the pairs to classify the questions on the board into sub-groups. Then have them share their categorisations.

9 Ask the students what makes one question "richer" than another.

Variation
Instead of doing this exercise about a picture, an object or a piece of music, use the reading passage in the current unit in your coursebook.

Note
It is rare in the EFL culture for students to formulate questions which never get answered; a breath of fresh air!

Acknowledgement
We adapted this exercise from page 39 of *Games for Thinking* by Robert Fisher, 1997, Nash Pollock Publishing.

Dynamic questions

Language focus	Asking questions, answering questions, intensive listening
Proposed MI focus	Interpersonal, intrapersonal and logical–mathematical
Level	Lower intermediate upwards
Time	30–40 minutes
Preparation	None.

in class

1 Ask each student to think of three questions they would like to be asked in front of the whole class. The questions should be "open" ones, ie not expecting Yes/No answers. Ask the students to write each of the questions legibly on a separate slip of paper in block letters, and so that others will not easily be able to guess who the writer is.

2 Ask them to put all the paper slips in a box.

3 Shuffle the paper slips and ask each student to draw a question.

4 Give them time to decide who in the group might have written the question they have drawn (by speculating who might like to be asked this question). Tell them to ask the person the question. This person should then answer the question. If they are not the person who wrote the question, they should nevertheless answer it as if they had written it.

5 When a question has been asked and answered, there is a silent time of about a minute. In this time, students should speculate as to whether the person who was asked the question is the one who had written it, and why or why not they think so. They should then make notes of their thoughts.

6 Get them to continue until everybody in the group has asked one question.

7 Ask the students to work in groups and compare their notes.

8 In a whole-class discussion, give students an opportunity to ask anything they would like to ask about the matter in hand, e.g. who had written a certain question.

Interactive loops for groups

Language focus	Listening for details, reading out aloud
Proposed MI focus	Interpersonal, linguistic
Level	Beginners upwards; the example given here is lower intermediate
Time	10 minutes
Preparation	Produce a set of cards for your own interactive loop game, or copy the cards on page 95 and cut them out.

in class

1 Give each pupil one card. If there are any cards left, give a few students a second card. If the number of students in your class exceeds the number of cards, produce more cards following the procedures described under *Making your own interactive loop game*, below.

2 Ask the students to read their cards, and to call you should they not know a meaning or a pronunciation.

3 Tell the students that any of them can start the game by reading out the question on their card. If the game is played correctly, the person who starts the game will also be the person to end it. Ask them to read loudly and clearly.

4 One student begins by reading out the question on their card. Whoever believes they have the answer reads it out from their card. If they're right, they then read out the question they have on their card. If they're not right, someone else tries reading out their answer.

5 The game is over as soon as all the questions and answers have been read out. It can be repeated as often as your students wish, by getting a student to collect the cards, shuffle them and hand them out again.

Variations

The loop game can be used in many ways to revise and practise:

Specific language areas, such as:

- synonyms/antonyms (e.g. What is a synonym for *friend*? Buddy. What's an antonym for *boring*? Exciting.)
- grammatical descriptions and structures (What's the superlative of *good*? Best.)
- definitions and words (e.g. What is meant by *claustrophobia*? An unpleasant feeling which some people get when they are in small, enclosed places.)
- questions and answers (e.g. *What did you do for your weekend? – I went sailing with Mario.*
NB Each question must have only one possible answer.)

Specific content areas, such as:
• a trivia quiz on the content of the stories in your coursebook.
• a cross curricular quiz on a subject area of your choice.
• a general knowledge quiz.

Making your own interactive loop game

You can tailor-make the loop game to any number of students in your class. Let's assume you have 25 students and you want to design for this class an interactive loop game that helps to practise synonyms/antonyms. Prepare 25 cards, each about 5 x 8 cm. Write a question in the lower part of the first card, e.g:

Card 1:

> What's the opposite of *ugly*?

Write the answer in the upper half of the second card, and another question in the lower half of the same card, e.g.:

Card 2:

> Beautiful.
> What's a synonym of *empty*?

Carry on like this with the rest of the cards. When you come to the question on Card 25, you write the answer to this question in the upper half of the first card. This completes the loop.

Variation

This simple technique can usefully be used in the language classroom, drawing on material from any of the other intelligences. Here are what some of these cards could look like in the mathematical area:

Example 1:

> **I have 3.**
> *Who has the square of this?*

> **I have 9.**
> *Who has the square root of this plus 2?*

> **I have 5.**
> *Who has the square of this?*

> **I have 25.**
> *Who has the square root of this minus 1?*

Example 2: (random cards)

I have an acute angle.
Who has an angle of more than 90 degrees?

I have an obtuse angle.
Who has the name for the distance around the outside of a circle?

Acknowledgement

The idea for this type of activity comes from *Think Math! Interactive Loops for Groups* by Dale Bulla, 1996, Zephyr Press, Tucson, Arizona.

Irregular verb forms interactive loop game:

Drove. What's the past form of *write*?	*Began.* What's the past participle of *know*?	*Wrote.* What's the base form of *went*?
Go. What's the past participle of *put*?	*Swum.* What's the base form of *understood*?	*Thought.* What's the past participle of *fight*?
Rose. What's the base form of *lain*?	*Understood.* What's the past participle of *swim*?	*Rode.* What's the past participle of *sing*?
Sing. What's the past form of *sing*?	*Begin.* What's the past form of *think*?	*Known.* What's the past form of *know*?
Found. What's the base form of *chosen*?	*Sang.* What's the past form of *begin*?	*Put.* What's the base form of *began*?
Fought. What's the past form of *risen*?	*Sung.* What's the base form of *sung*?	*Lie.* What's the past participle of *find*?
Knew. What's the past form of *understand*.	*Choose.* What's the past form of *ride*?	*Understand.* What's the past form of *drive?*

© Helbling Languages 2005. Please photocopy this page for use in class.

Speculating

Language focus	Writing and listening
Proposed MI focus	Interpersonal and intrapersonal
Level	Lower intermediate upwards
Time	15–20 minutes
Preparation	None.

in class

1 Ask your learners if they know a person who seems to be good at guessing what goes on in other people's minds. Ask them to give an example of an experience with such a person.

2 Ask your learners to work with a partner. Get them to write down three sentences about their partner that are speculations about that person. Tell them not to share the speculations yet. If you like, you can give them a thematic frame for their guesses, e.g. their childhood. You may want to give them a few examples:

I think you were your parents' only child and you got all the love and attention from them.

I think it was very important for your mother that you were always dressed neatly.

Possibly your father was interested in sports and taught you various sports. He was proud of you when you won a competition.

3 Tell the students that the A's in each group will close their eyes, while their partner will slowly read out their speculation to them. After each statement, there is a short pause to allow the listener to reflect. When all the three statements have been read out, the listeners open their eyes to note down their thoughts.

4 The pairs swap roles.

5 When the pairs have finished, give them about five minutes to share their notes and their feelings during the activity.

Note
This is a very personal exercise. It draws on and helps develop empathy with others, the ability to "put oneself into someone else's shoes". It is best used when students know each other reasonably well.

Spatialising language

Language focus	Guessing phrases and words by deriving cues from spatalisation
Proposed MI focus	Spatial, linguistic, logical
Level	Intermediate upwards
Time	15 minutes
Preparation	One copy of the handout (page 100) per pair of students.

in class

1 Write the following letter puzzles on the board. Do not say anything, but wait for your students to start guessing what they may mean:

YY UR,

YY UB.

I C U R

YY 4 Me!

Solution:
Too wise you are,
too wise you be.
I see you are
too wise for me!

Give them a copy of the handout on page 100. Get them to work in pairs or small groups, to try to figure out the expression that each picture represents. Ask them not to immediately call out an expression once they have found it.

Then get your students to compare their findings. Check if anybody has found solutions different from the ones you can offer. Then get them to think of other expressions that they could represent spatially. Ask them to create images for expressions such as *It's water under the bridge* or *Flying colours,* which have double meanings, and ask them to draw the visual representations of these expressions in the empty frames. Students interested in this sort of puzzle activity may want to create their own for one of the next classes.

Solution to handout:
1 circles under the eyes
2 love at first sight
3 standing ovations
4 that's beside the point!
5 microwave
6 high income brackets
7 sitting on top of the world
8 hands up!
9 double-decker bus
10 washing up
11 more often than not

Acknowledgement

We have learnt some of the spatialisations of language presented here from a colleague in Munich, Rolf Preller. Others come in the work of D. Loomas and K. Kolberg, *The Laughing Classroom*, 1993, H. J. Kramer Inc.

1 i i i i O O O O	**2** sight love sight sight	**3** O V A T I O N S	**4** .that's
5 	**6** [INCOME]	**7** sitting world	
8 DD NN AA HH	**9** BUS BUS	**10** G N I H S A W	**11** often not often not often

© Helbling Languages 2005. Please photocopy this page for use in class.

Spatial metaphor

Language focus	Speaking (political and economic discussion)
Proposed MI focus	Spatial and logical–mathematical
Level	Lower intermediate to advanced
Time	20–30 minutes
Preparation	Make two photocopies of the tree (page 102) for each student.

in class

1 Ask the students to work alone and to write a list of as many of the provinces, autonomous regions or states in their own country as they can.

2 Give each student a copy of the tree and ask them to write in the names of their provinces or states on the symbolically appropriate figures in the tree branches or on the ground. They do this individually, as well.

3 Bring the students together in groups of five or six, and ask them to explain to each other why they associated this or that area of their country with this or that figure on the tree.

4 If your class all belong to the same country, ask them to make a list of 10–15 other countries in the surrounding region. If the students in your class are international, ask them to list all the countries their classmates come from, plus one country that borders on each.

5 Give each student a new copy of the tree picture and ask them to associate the countries on their list with different figures in the tree.

6 The students come together in groups of five to six, and explain within their group the reasons for their placings.

Exemplification
When we did this exercise with a group of Italian doctoral sociologists, they came out with a flood of language to try and explain why several of them had put Germany as the central figure at the top and why many of them had seen UK as the top right-hand figure. A couple of people saw a seated, waving figure at the centre top as Ireland. This exercise really freed up the participants' language on Day 2 of their six-day total-immersion course.

Variation
You can use this tree picture to get umpteen discussions going; here are some
suggestions:
With a group of historians: the presidents of the USA
With a group of chemists: the elements from the periodic table
With a group of architects: buildings and spaces in the local town
With anybody: members of the extended family; teachers and students in a school; colleagues in a workplace etc.

Acknowledgement
We learnt this flexible frame from a Pilgrims colleague, Penelope Williams.

© Helbling Languages 2005. Please photocopy this page for use in class.

CHAPTER 3: LOOKING OUT

Animal quiz

Language focus	Intensive reading, spelling, homophones and homonyms
Proposed MI focus	Linguistic
Level	Intermediate to advanced
Time	Lesson 1: 5 minutes Lesson 2: 10–15 minutes
Preparation	Copy one questionnaire per student (see page 104).

in class

Lesson 1

1 Write up this question on the board:
Which European country has a name very similar to the word for a large sea animal?
Give the students a moment to puzzle it out and then draw a map of the UK. This should help them to get Wales/whales.

2 Give them the questionnaire for homework and suggest they get help from someone they know who is good at English. They also may want to ring up classmates.

Lesson 2

1 Find out which questions they were able to answer, and which ones had foxed them. Give them any answers they did not get.

Solution to the Animal Questionnaire (page 104):

1	deer/dear	11	bear/bare
2	ewe/yew	12	mouse
3	calf	13	to duck/duck
4	mayor/mare	14	to rat on/a rat
5	to hawk/a hawk	15	dough/dough (money)/doe
6	bitch	16	cheetah/cheater (which really is cheating!)
7	place/plaice	17	hare/hair
8	bat	18	seal
9	bull	19	to badger a person for something/a badger
10	to fox	20	aunt/ant

Animal Questionnaire

1   Something is expensive; you love someone – which animal do you think of?
2   A personal pronoun that sounds the same as an animal and a tree in a graveyard.
3   Which young animal has a name that is also part of the human leg?
4   Think of a leading person of a city that sounds like a female animal.
5   A verb meaning "sell" which is the same word as a bird of prey.
6   Can you think of a very derogatory word for a woman and a puppy's mum?
7   This word for a location sounds the same as the name of a fish.
8   What animal navigates by sonar and is something that's useful in some ball games?
9   What big animal tells you that the stock market is optimistic?
10 An idea is unclear to you; it is beyond you – what does it do to you that is like the name of a clever animal?
11 What furry animal sounds the same as an adjective meaning "without clothes"?
12 A rodent that nests near a computer?
13 If some one tries to hit you, you do something that is the same word as a water bird.
14 A person betrays you or lets you down. Part of this verb phrase is also the name of a rodent.
15 You knead it, you need it and it lives in the forest.
16 This word makes you think of a swift animal and dishonesty.
17 A bald person does not have this animal.
18 It's something a king used to have, and the animal lives in cold water.
19 You keep on demanding things, and the animal has a white streak down its face.
20 In the American way of speaking, this is a relative and an insect.

© Helbling Languages 2005. Please photocopy this page for use in class.

The truth about me

Language focus	Writing, speaking
Proposed MI focus	Interpersonal and intrapersonal, logical
Level	Lower intermediate to intermediate
Time	40 minutes
Preparation	None.

in class

1 Get each student to write six sentences about themselves. Two to four of these sentences should be lies.

2 Put the students into groups of four. One student starts dictating to their group the sentences that he or she has written. The student tells the others how many of his or her sentences are lies – but not which ones.

3 The students discuss the sentences, to decide which of them they believe are true and which are lies, and why.

4 They then tell the person who has given the dictation what they think about the sentences, and they give their reasons for this. The person listens, but does not comment. Only when they have finished their report does the person reveal which the lies are. The others now also get a chance to ask questions.

5 Ask the students to repeat the above steps three times, so that each student has a turn to dictate their true/false statements.

Variation
It is especially popular with younger students if you write sentences about yourself on the board. Students often want to get to know their teacher better, and this game offers an excellent opportunity. From a psychological point of view, the game is interesting because it enables learners to realise their own projections about the teacher and to compare these with the teacher's reality.

Acknowledgement
We learnt this activity from Philip Prowse.

How many questions a minute?

Language focus Question formation

Proposed MI focus Interpersonal and intrapersonal

Level Lower intermediate to advanced

Time 10 minutes

Preparation None.

in class

1 Explain the complete procedure for the activity first (for this description, A is female and B is male):

Students work in pairs. Partner A asks B as many questions as she can within one minute. B does not answer any of the questions immediately.

When the minute is over, there is a short silence to allow B to try and remember the questions. He should now answer as many of the questions as he can, and among the answers he gives, he should tell one lie.

A watches and listens to B giving the answers, and when she thinks she has spotted the lie, she should remember it, but does not immediately tell B.

When B has finished answering all the questions he has remembered/wanted to answer, A and B swap roles.

2 Afterwards, give the pairs a few minutes to tell each other what they think the lies were, and how they noticed them.

Acknowledgement
The idea of getting learners to spot each other's manipulations of reality has been used in many classrooms very successfully. We first learnt it from Andrew Wright.

50 Handing a word round the circle

Language focus	In Part 1: spontaneous vocabulary work In Part 2: intonations and sounds
Proposed MI focus	Giving sounds, words and phrases a grounding in kinaesthetic area of reality
Level	Post beginner to advanced
Time	Part 1: 15–20 minutes Part 2: 10 minutes
Preparation	None.

in class

Part 1

1 All this happens with the students silent:

Ask the learners to stand in a circle. (If you have a large class, get half of them into the standing circle, and the other half sitting round the inside of the circle, watching.) Get one person to **imagine** they are holding an object. They do not say what it is. They feel its weight, feel its temperature. They feel its surface. Now they pass it to the person on their right, who holds out their hands to receive it.

This person can either pass the object on as she thinks it is, or can change it.

The next person receives it, etc.

2 Get a student to note down on the board any words that are new to the group. Then ask the first person to tell the group what they gave to their neighbour.

The second person is then to say:

I received a ...

...and then I gave him/her a...

Tell the students it's OK if what they receive is different from what they have been given.

3 Continue until all the students in the circle have said what they got and what they gave.

Part 2

1 Now explain that they are going to play a similar game, but this time with words or phrases. Cupping your hands and mentally "holding the word in your hands", physically give the word and say it loud and clear to your neighbour in the circle. They turn "with the word in their hands" and give it to the next person, and so on round the group.

2 As the word or phrase goes round, it may get mispronounced. If this happens, go downstream of the error and with your cupped hands take it back from the next person and give the word to someone upstream of the person who's made the mistake. Do this gently and glidingly, without looking at the person who got it wrong. If they get it wrong again, let it pass.

Note

We have used this exercise to deal with areas of intonation and sound that learners find hard, e.g.: *Z'a man at the door*, rather than the extended form:

There is a man…

If you teach Italians or Spaniards, try using a phrase like *Happy Harry*.
If you teach Japanese, use: *What a funny face*.

Spatial jokes

Language focus	Listening (understanding punch lines) and speaking
Proposed MI focus	Spatial and logical–mathematical
Level	Intermediate
Time	20–30 minutes
Preparation	Make copies of the joke sheet (page 110). If you like telling jokes, prepare to tell the ones below.

in class

1 Either tell the class the jokes, or hand them the joke sheet to read.

2 Ask them to vote on which jokes they liked best and which they liked least.

3 Dictate these questions to the group:
When you read or heard the jokes, what sort of places came to mind?
When you were looking at these places, were you a spectator or part of the scene?
Which places had the strongest feeling for you?

They answer the questions in groups of four or five.

4 Ask them to translate the joke they liked best, to try out on the folks at home

Joke sheet

A: Good afternoon. Can you help me?

B: Well, maybe I can, sorr.

A: How can I get onto the Dublin road from here?

B: The Dublin road ... er ... well it's not that easy, starting from here, sorr. If I was you, I wouldn't start from here.

This lorry driver came to a low bridge. He stopped and wondered if his truck would get through. He really wasn't sure – it could only be a matter of centimetres.

A local man had been watching him:

"Why don't you let the tyres down a tad? There's a petrol station just the other side of the bridge – you can blow them up again there."

"No way," says the driver, "See, I got a problem at the top, not the bottom!"

The general is inspecting the troops. He stops in front of this soldier: "How do you make a cannon?"
"Sir! You takes a hole and you puts the metal round it."

I was working in my field halfway up the hill when I saw a police jeep reversing up the slope.

"What are you doing that for?" I asked.

"We're not sure if there is space to turn," the policeman said, "up at the top there."

Quarter of an hour later I saw them coming back down the hill, still in reverse.

I couldn't believe my eyes. "How come?" I asked them.
"Simple," said the driver, "there was plenty of turning space at the top, so we took advantage of it."

I stopped this man on a bicycle and asked him the way to Braithwaite.

"Ah," he said, "it's close by. You don't have a great way to go, now. You go straight down the road here and you take a right turn about 300 yards <u>before</u> you get to see the Braithwaite church tower.

© Helbling Languages 2005. Please photocopy this page for use in class.

Musical experiences

Language focus	Speaking about past experiences
Proposed MI focus	Musical, interpersonal
Level	Lower intermediate to advanced
Time	10–20 minutes
Preparation	Be ready to tell the group about three musical experiences of yours.

in class

1 Tell the students about three musical moments in your life.

2 Ask them to work in threes, and share three musical moments of their own.

Variation
Do the same exercise with another intelligence area, e.g. intrapersonal.
A possible instruction could be:
*Tell your partners about three moments when you were really happy
to be on your own – tell them how you made the moment enjoyable.*

Acknowledgement
We learnt this activity from Clement Laroy during a workshop in Brussels.

A new angle on my way home?

Language focus	Language of geometry
Proposed MI focus	Spatial and logical–mathematical
Level	Lower intermediate to advanced
Time	20–30 minutes
Preparation	None.

in class

1 Ask your students to imagine themselves leaving their school, university or workplace, and setting out on their way home. Ask them to jot down how many left turns they make, and how many right turns.

2 Ask them to draw a diagram of their route home, noting all angles of all the bends and turns on the way. Ask them to notice that some angles are acute and others are obtuse (more than 90°). Ask them to write in the approximate number of degrees. If their path, road, railtrack or underground track curves, ask them to estimate the angle of the entire turn.

3 Now ask them to mark 5–10 landmarks onto their route.

4 Group the students in threes. Ask one of the students to describe their route, while the others listen with their eyes closed. After this blind listening they will really want to look at the diagram.

5 The other two students in each trio describe their routes home in the same way.

Note
Some students may never have thought of their route home in geometric terms. If a person thinks in a fresh way about something extremely well-known to them, this will normally enrich the subsequent description of it.

Numbers that are mine

Language focus	Collocations that include number
Proposed MI focus	Logical–mathematical, intrapersonal and interpersonal
Level	Post-beginner to intermediate
Time	20–30 minutes
Preparation	Prepare to enumerate numbers that have been, or are, important in your life. To get you thinking, here are some numbers that are important to Mario:

244 phone number in my first home
57 this was my identification number in boarding school; even my shoes were stamped with the figure 57!
0223 this was the phone code for Cambridge in the 70s and 80s – I lived there for 27 years
1940 my birth year
6 and 8 because I like their rounded shapes
4 even though the Japanese think it unlucky, it has always been a good number for me
33 Kinnaird Way – my house number in Cambridge
15 20 Picarte quince-veinte – my house number in Chile
504 Decreto quinientos cuatro – Decree 504 – allowed many of my friends to get out of their Chilean prisons and carry their intelligence abroad
26 November 1994 date I moved house
9 miles distance from my home to my work
95 kilos my weight
35 mph my Honda moped's maximum speed downhill with a following wind!

in class

1 Tell the class about numbers that are special to you.

2 Group them in fours to tell each other about their special numbers.

Human camera

Language focus	Visual description
Proposed MI focus	Kinaesthetic, spatial and linguistic
Level	Lower to upper intermediate
Time	10–20 minutes
Preparation	Check that the students' cultures permits them to rest their hands on one another's shoulders.

1 If possible, work outdoors. Pair the students. (For this description, A is male and B is female.)

2 Tell them that person A is the photographer and Person B is the "camera". B stands up with her eyes shut, and A stands behind her, resting his hands on her shoulders.

A steers B around the space available, and when he wants to take photograph gets his camera into the right position, then takes the photo by pressing her shoulder. B opens her eyes for three seconds and takes in and remembers exactly what she sees.

3 A takes three photos using B as camera. Then they switch roles, and B uses A as her camera.

4 When the students come back, ask them all to draw rough outlines on paper of the three pictures they took when they were cameras.

5 Group the students in sixes and have the cameras describe to the rest of the group as accurately as they can what their lenses saw.

Acknowledgement
We learnt this activity in Peta Grey's workshop at an International House conference.

56 Starting a group

Language focus	Listening and speaking about own experience
Proposed MI focus	Interpersonal
Level	Elementary to advanced
Time	20–30 minutes (with teenagers) 30–40 minutes (with adults)
Preparation	Be ready to talk about a "good" group and a "bad"* group you have taught.

in class

1 Tell the students about a class you have taught who you reckon were a good group. Explain what pleased you about this group.

2 Ask the students to work in groups of fours, and ask each person in the foursome to describe a good group they have been in, whether in school or elsewhere.

3 Bring the whole class back together. Ask one person from each foursome to describe to the class the good group that had been described by someone else in his or her group.

4 Tell the students about a bad group you have worked with.

5 In their fours, the students tell each other about a bad group they have been in. Tell them that you won't be holding whole-group discussion on this, and that their opinions will stay private to their foursome.

6 Ask the students each to write you a paragraph about their expectations about this particular class/group, for the class to see. Collect these together, read them and, before the next lesson, post them on a wall of the classroom.

* My "bad" group may be your "good" group; you may feel that intra-group conflict is evidence of honesty, while I may be one of those teachers who find conflict negative. This is why we have put "good" and "bad" in inverted commas.

Note
We suggest you do *not* have whole-group feedback after the foursome work on the bad groups, as students will often be speaking of bad teachers… to discuss this in the class plenary could be embarrassing for both them and you.

CHAPTER 4
LOOKING IN

Imaging

Language focus	Reading
Proposed MI focus	Linguistic, spatial
Level	Lower intermediate upwards
Time	Lesson 1: 10 minutes Lesson 2: 30–40 minutes
Preparation	Photocopy one of the sample texts below. Sample Text A (page 121) is for lower intermediate students. Sample Text B (page 123) is for advanced students. Alternatively, select a text appropriate for your class, and create questions stimulating sensory imagination as in the models below.

in class

Lesson 1

1 Write the following sentence on the board:
I looked at the waves and as I heard the sound of the water I could feel the warm sand under my feet.

2 Say this:

I'd like you to read this sentence and then either close your eyes or look somewhere else. Imagine that you are experiencing this situation right now. Allow your imagination to create the situation described in the sentence as vividly as possible. Focus on what you can hear, see and feel. You can take your time to do this.

3 Ask your students whether they found it easier to imagine things visually, hear sounds or voices, or access feelings. It is important that you show a non-judgmental attitude. Some students might say that, for example, they find it very difficult to see pictures in their mind's eye whereas they find it easy to hear sounds, so make it clear that this is perfectly normal.

4 Tell your class that they are going to do a similar activity in the next lesson, based on a longer text. Tell them that they are going to be given a text and suggestions that will help them to activate their imagination while reading it. Say that they should not rush, as there will be enough time for them to fully experience and enjoy the images stimulated by the text.

Lesson 2

1 Give out the text. Whenever they have read the text as far as an instruction they should read that instruction. Then they should go back to the text again, and allow themselves to be stimulated by the part of the text that the instruction refers to. Remind them of the activity you did in the previous lesson. Tell them that they should either close their eyes or look somewhere else, and allow up to a minute for each visualisation.

2 Allow enough time for your learners to go through the text as described above.

3 Ask your learners, in pairs or small groups, to share their favourite moment or image stimulated by the text.

Note

People with a high ability to form images while reading are able to recall and recognise more items from the text than low imagers. This activity aims to help learners develop their ability to use their senses while they are reading, and possibly form visual images. The activity may also help students to appreciate the literary quality of a text more fully.

Acknowledgement

We learnt about the story of *Cornelia, the Panda Princess* from Günter Gerngross. The other text is taken from *The Education of Little Tree*, Forrest Carter, 1976, University of New Mexico Press, Albuquerque, pages 6–11 (abbreviated).

While you are reading text A do this:

Imagine you can see Princess Cornelia in front of you with her crown sparkling in the light.

Imagine you can see the King looking at his daughter and hear him talking loudly to her.

Imagine that you can see and hear Cornelia entering the cave and then hear the Wise Man's soft voice.

Imagine the situation on the mountain. Cornelia is waking up. Hear the birds and see the sun rise. Feel the warmth of the sun on your skin.

Sample Text A

Princess Cornelia was a panda. She was the most beautiful panda in China. She had big black eyes, soft and shiny black and white fur, and a charming smile. She wore a golden crown on her head full of diamonds and rubies which sparkled in the light

The princess had a friend. His name was Frederick. He was a panda, too, and he was extremely handsome. Cornelia loved Frederick, and he loved her. She wanted to marry him, and he wanted to marry her. But Cornelia's father, King Simon, was against the idea of this marriage. He told her that she could not marry a panda.

"Why not, father? I love Frederick. I want to marry him, and he wants to marry me," she said.

The King looked fiercely at his daughter and answered in a very loud voice: "You're a panda princess, and a panda princess cannot marry a panda. You must marry the strongest creature in the world."

The Princess did not know what to do, so she went to see a Wise Man who lived in a cave in the forest. She was very frightened as she made her way along the forest paths. When she entered the cave, it was very quiet. The only noise she could hear was the sound of her footsteps and the dripping of water on the rocks. It was very dark inside the cave and she found it difficult to see anything. Suddenly she heard the Wise Man's soft voice: "What can I do for you, Princess Cornelia?"

Cornelia explained that she was looking for the strongest creature in the world, but did not know where to find him. The Wise Man thought for a few moments and then answered: "The strongest creature is the sun. There is no creature in the whole universe that is stronger than the sun."

"Then please tell me how I can find him," said Cornelia.

"You must go a long way. He lives behind the highest mountain in the land," answered the Wise Man.

So Cornelia set off to find the sun. After a very long walk Cornelia reached the mountain.

Then she began climbing up the steep slopes. When night fell she was halfway up the mountain, and too tired to continue. So she lay down on a flat rock and fell fast asleep. In the morning she was woken by the singing of hundreds of birds and as she opened her eyes she could see the beautiful golden rays of the sun rising above the rocks. After the cold night on the mountain it was wonderful to feel the warmth of the sun. She called out to him: "My father, King Simon, says I must marry the strongest creature in the world. And the Wise Man in the forest has told me that that is you."

"Oh no, Cornelia," said the sun, and laughed. "I'm not the strongest creature. You should go to the cloud. He can stop me shining whenever he wants to. Look, here he comes now."

© Helbling Languages 2005. Please photocopy this page for use in class.

See the great flash of lightning; hear the thunder and rain up on the mountain.

At that moment the sun disappeared. There was a great flash of lightning and a roll of thunder and rain began pouring down onto the mountainside. Cornelia called out to the dark cloud above her: "Cloud! Can you hear me?"

A deep voice came from the cloud above her, speaking very slowly: "Yes, Princess. What do you want?"

"My father, King Simon, says I must marry the strongest creature in the world. And the sun told me that that is you."

The cloud laughed. "I'm not the strongest creature. The wind is the strongest. He can blow me away whenever he wants to."

Hear the howling of the wind and see Cornelia clinging onto the rocks.

Suddenly there was a howling and whistling in Cornelia's ears as the wind blew the cloud away. She had to hang onto the rocks to stop herself being blown away too. "Wind! Wind!" she called out above the terrible noise.

Gradually the wind became quieter and at last he spoke: "What is it? Who is calling me when I am busy doing my work?"

"It's me, down here!" called out Cornelia. "I'm Princess Cornelia. "My father, King Simon, says I must marry the strongest creature in the world. And the cloud told me that that is you."

The wind laughed. "I'm not the strongest creature. The bamboo is the strongest. I have tried again and again, but I can never break him."

Hear the sounds of the forest and the swishing of the bamboo.

So Cornelia climbed back down the mountain and made her way back into the forest. As she was walking along the forest path she heard leaves rustling all around her and then at last she heard the swishing of the bamboo.

"Bamboo," she called out, "My father, King Simon, says I must marry the strongest creature in the world. And the wind told me that that is you."

The bamboo laughed. "I'm not the strongest creature. Frederick, the panda, is the strongest."

The princess was astonished. "Frederick? Frederick is stronger than you? Why?"

"Because he can eat me," answered the bamboo.

So Cornelia went back to her father, the Panda King, and told him the story.

Imagine you are taking part in the wedding celebrations. See the beautiful colours, hear the music and the people, and experience the joy and happiness.

Six weeks later the palace was full of happy music and the joyful sounds of people celebrating. People dressed in colourful clothes were dancing in the streets and everywhere there were flags and garlands of flowers. The King had given his permission for Cornelia and Frederick to be married and now he was very happy about it too.

© Helbling Languages 2005. Please photocopy this page for use in class.

While you are reading text B do this:

Sample Text B

This story is an extract from the novel *The Education of Little Tree* by Forrest Carter. Little Tree is an Indian boy who is brought up by his grandparents after his parents have died.

This morning I slipped the moccasins on last, after I had jumped into my overalls and buttoned my jacket. It was dark and cold – too early even for the morning whisper wind to stir the trees.

Grandpa had said I could go with him on the high trail, if I got up, and he had said that he would not wake me.

Imagine the situation when Little Tree wakes up and hears the noises that his grandfather is making.

"A man rises of his own will in the morning," he had spoken down to me and he did not smile. But Grandpa had made many noises in his rising, bumping the wall of my room and talking uncommonly loud to Grandma, and so I had heard, and so I had heard, and I was first out, waiting with the hounds in the darkness.

"So. Ye're here," Grandpa sounded surprised.

"Yes, sir," I said and kept the proud out of my voice.

Grandpa pointed his finger at the hounds jumping and prancing around us. "Ye'll stay," he ordered, and they tucked in their tails and whined and begged and ol' Maud set up a howl. But they didn't follow us. They stood, all together in a hopeless little bunch, and watched as leave the clearing.

Imagine that you are Little Tree walking up the icy trail.
You are breathing out in the cold air and your breath becomes visible.

The cold air steamed my breath in clouds and the spring branch fell far below us. Bare tree branches dripped water from ice prongs that teethed their sides, and as we walked higher there was ice on the trail. Grey light eased the darkness away. Grandpa stopped and pointed by the side of the trail. "There she is – turkey run – see?" I dropped to my hands and knees and saw the tracks: little sticklike impressions coming out from a center hub.

"Now," Grandpa said, "we'll fix the trap." And he moved off the trail until he found a stump hole.

We cleaned it out, first the leaves, and then Grandpa pulled out his long knife and cut into the spongy ground and we scooped up the dirt, scattering it among the leaves.

When the hole was deep, so that I couldn't see over the rim, Grandpa pulled me out and we dragged tree branches to cover it and, over these, spread armful of leaves. Then, with his long knife, Grandpa dug a trail sloping downward into the hole and back toward the turkey run. He took the grains of red Indian corn from his pocket and scattered them down the trail, and threw a handful into the hole.

"Now we will go," he said, and set off again up the high trail. Ice, spewed from the earth like frosting, crackled under our feet. The mountain opposite us moved closer as the hollow far below became a narrow slit, showing the spring branch like the edge of a steel knife, sunk into the bottom of its cleavage.

© Helbling Languages 2005. Please photocopy this page for use in class.

Imagine the sun rising over the top of the mountain. Experience the feelings that the boy and his grandfather are having as they are eating their sour biscuits and deer meat watching the mountain.

We sat down in the leaves, off the trail, just as the first sun touched the top of the mountains across the hollow. From his pocket, Grandpa pulled out a sour biscuit and dear meat for me, and we watched the mountain while we ate.

The sun hit the top like an explosion, sending showers of glitter and sparkle into the air. The sparkling of the icy trees hurt the eyes to look, and it moved down the mountain line a wave as the sun backed the night shadow down and down.

There were no clouds but at first I didn't see the speck that came over the rim. It grew larger. Facing into the sun, so that the shadow did not go before him, the bird sped down the side of the mountain, a skier on the tree-tops, wings half-folded ... like a brown bullet ... faster and faster, toward the quails.

Grandpa chuckled, "It's ol' Tal-con, the hawk."

Visualise how the hawk speeds down the side of the mountain and catches the quail.

The quails rose in a rush and sped into the trees – but one was slow. The hawk hit. Feathers flew in the air and then the birds were on the ground, the hawk's head rising and falling with the death blows. In a moment he rose with the dead quail clutched in his claws, back up the side of the mountain and over the rim.

Imagine that you are Little Tree's grandfather who notices that his grandson looks sad because the hawk has killed the quail. Focus on what 'you' are feeling as 'you' are explaining to Little Tree that this is The Way.

I didn't cry, but I know I looked sad, because Grandpa said, "Don't feel sad, Little Tree. It is The Way. Tal-con caught the slow and so the slow will raise no children who are also slow. Tal-con eats a thousand ground rats who eat the eggs of the quail – both the quick and the slow eggs – and so Tal-con lives by The Way. He helps the quail."

"It is The Way," he said softly. "Take only what ye need. When ye take the deer, do not take the best. Take the smaller and the slower and then the deer will grow stronger and always give you meat. Pa-koh, the panther, knows and so must ye."

And he laughed, "Only Ti-bi, the bee, stores more than he can use ... and so he is robbed by the bear, and the 'coon... and the Cherokee. It is so with people who store and fat themselves with more than their share. They will have it taken from them. And there will be wars over it ... and they will make long talks, trying to hold more than their share. They will say a flag stands for their right to do this ... and men will die because of the words and the flag, but they will not change the rules of The Way."

We went back down the trail, and the sun was high over us when we reached the turkey trap. We could hear them before we saw the trap. They were in there, gobbling and making loud whistles of alarm.

Imagine you are standing by the turkey trap. Listen to the noises the turkeys are making.

Grandpa stretched full length into the hole and pulled out a big squawking turkey, tied his legs with a throng and grinned at me.

Grandpa pulled out some more turkeys, laid them out on the ground, legs tied. There were six of them, and now he pointed down at them. "They're all about the same age, ye can tell by the thickness of the combs. We only need three so now ye choose, Little Tree."

© Helbling Languages 2005. Please photocopy this page for use in class.

Imagine you are Little Tree. Experience yourself walking around the turkeys and finally pulling out the three smallest you can find.

I walked around them, flopping on the ground. I squatted and studied them, and walked around them again. I had to be careful. I got down on my hands and knees, and crawled among them, until I had pulled out the three smallest I could find.

Grandpa said nothing. He pulled the throngs from the legs of the others and they took to wing, beating down the side of the mountain. He slung two of the turkey over his shoulder. "Can ye carry the other?" he asked.

"Yes, sir," I said, not sure that I had done right. A slow grin broke Grandpa's bony face. "If ye was not Little Tree ... I would call ye Little Hawk."

Imagine you are Little Tree. Feel the weight of the turkey on your shoulder asyou are following your grandfather down the trail. See the golden patterns that the sun creates when it is shining through the branches of the trees. Listen to Grandpa humming a tune and feel what it is like to have learned The Way.

I followed Grandpa down the trail. The turkey was heavy, but it felt good over my shoulder. The sun had tilted toward the father mountains and drifted through the branches of the trees beside the trail, making burnt golden patterns where we walked. The wind had died in that late afternoon of winter, and I heard Grandpa, ahead of me, humming a tune. I would have liked to live that time forever ... for I knew I had pleased Grandpa. I had learnt The Way.

© Helbling Languages 2005. Please photocopy this page for use in class.

Listening with your mind's eye

Language focus   Listening and speaking

Proposed MI focus   Spatial and linguistic

Level   Lower intermediate to advanced. The example given here is for use with intermediate students.

Time   5–10 minutes

Preparation   Select a poem or any other text suitable for your class that is likely to stimulate the students' visual and spatial imagination. Alternatively, use the poem on page 127.

in class

In class

1 Tell your students that you are going to read out a text to them. Ask them to listen with their eyes closed, and focus on what they see, hear, feel etc. while you are reading. Tell them that some of them may be mainly seeing clear and colourful pictures, while others will probably be able to "get a feel for visual images", but may see only very blurred pictures or no pictures at all.

2 Quietly ask the students to work in small groups and to share their favourite moments during their experience of the poem.

Note

If you decide to use the poem by Jacques Prévert (page 127), tell your class that you are going to read out a poem to them which is almost like a set of instructions for painting a picture. Encourage them close their eyes and "paint" a picture in the air while they are listening to the instructions. Tell them that at one point in the poem, where there are no instructions to paint, they may feel like letting their arm sink down, but that they should start painting again as soon as the instructions to paint resume.

Acknowledgement

Jim Wingate introduced us to this technique. We also heard the Jacques Prévert poem for the first time in one of Jim's workshops.

To Paint the Portrait of a Bird

First paint a cage
with an open door
Then paint
something pretty
something simple
something beautiful
something useful
for the bird
Then place the canvas against a tree
in a garden
in a wood
or in a forest
Hide behind the tree
without speaking
without moving...
Sometimes the bird comes quickly
but it can just as well spend long years before deciding
Don't get discouraged
Wait
wait years if necessary
the swiftness or slowness
of the coming
of the bird having no rapport
with the success of the picture
When the bird comes
if it comes
observe the most profound silence
wait till the bird enters the cage
and when it has entered
gently close the door with a brush
Then
paint out all the bars one by one
taking care not to touch any of the
feathers of the bird
Then paint the portrait of the tree
choosing the most beautiful of its branches
for the bird
Paint also the green foliage and
the wind's freshness
the dust of the sun
and the noise of the insects in the summer heat
and then wait for the bird to decide to sing
If the bird doesn't sing
it's a bad sign –
a sign that the painting is bad
But if it sings it's a good sign
a sign that you can sign
So then so very gently you pull out
one of the feathers of the bird
and you write your name in the corner of the picture.

Jacques Prévert
(Translated by Lawrence Ferlinghetti)

© Helbling Languages 2005. Please photocopy this page for use in class.

Concentration on language

Language focus	Reading and speaking
Proposed MI focus	Linguistic, intrapersonal, interpersonal
Level	Lower intermediate upwards (the sample text is for intermediate)
Time	10 minutes
Preparation	Select a sentence or a short poem; use either the example on page 129, or your own. Make one copy of the poem per student.

in class

1 If space permits, ask the students to individually choose a place to sit where they feel they will not be easily disturbed by others. If a class is not used to working in intrapersonal mode, you may want to suggest to them that they sit facing the classroom wall.

2 Give out the text and ask the students to read it silently.

3 When they have done this, explain to them that listening and reading in L2 is much easier when they get into a state of relaxed concentration.
Today you are going to show them a technique they may also find useful before an exam. Invite them to close their eyes for a few minutes and take a few deep breaths to relax. Ask them to focus their attention on their body sensations, e.g. to become aware of the feeling of temperature in their body.

4 After two or three minutes tell them to open their eyes again and turn their full attention to the text in front of themselves. Invite them to focus on the text with an open and clear mind, without analysing it.

5 Tell them they should not worry if they get distracted. If their attention starts to wander, they should simply notice their thoughts, put them gently aside and come back to the text again.

6 Round this exercise off after four minutes or so with each student silently reflecting on their process of focusing attention.
Then initiate a discussion on this in pairs, groups or the whole class.

Note
The ability to focus one's attention and learn how to hold it for a longer span of time is an important skill that intrapersonally strong people usually have. It is also a cognitive skill that psychologists claim forms an important basis for the development of a number of so-called higher-order skills, like categorising and critical thinking. See for example Robert Fisher's excellent book, *Teaching Children to Think*, Stanley Thornes, 1992, Cheltenham.

Magic

There must be magic,
Otherwise,
How could day turn into night?
And how could sailboats,
Otherwise,
Go sailing out of sight?
And how could peanuts,
Otherwise,
Be covered up so tight?

© Helbling Languages 2005. Please photocopy this page for use in class.

Intrapersonal questionnaires

Language focus   Interrogative forms

Proposed MI focus   Intrapersonal and interpersonal
The exercise mode is strictly intrapersonal, though the thinking is about interpersonality.

Level   Lower intermediate to advanced

Time   10–15 minutes

Preparation   None.

in class

1 Explain to the learners that you are going to dictate a questionnaire to them but that there will be no discussion of the answers to the questions after the writing phase; you will be moving on directly to other work.

2 Dictate the questions and leave a half-minute silence after the last one before moving the lesson on.

Questionnaire on repeaters (for use at the start of the school year)
- *Where are all my classmates from last year?*
- *Aren't these people a great deal younger than me?*
- *Is it going to be all the same? Same text book, same homework, same teacher, same jokes?*
- *How many of this lot think I'm thick?*
- *Maybe I'll make new friends.*
- *Why have they dumped these repeaters in my class?*
- *I wonder how they feel about being here?*
- *They are older than us – will that make the teacher treat us all better?*

Questionnaire on noisy versus shy students
- *Should I try and speak more?*
- *Is there really any need to speak when I don't want to say anything?*
- *Does the teacher notice I don't often open my mouth?*
- *I wonder why I feel better speaking in a small group?*
- *Do some people feel I talk too much in this class?*
- *If I spoke less would others speak more?*
- *Do I speak more in English lessons than in other subjects?*
- *Doesn't the teacher talk a lot?*

Note
There are times when a teacher wants to make the students realise that he or she is aware of something and feels the students should be too, but does not feel that an open discussion by the class of the issue or issues would be useful. In this situation, *Intrapersonal Questionnaires* are a handy tool. We offer you a couple here, but the best ones will be the ones you produce yourself for specific situations. Another useful tool in this area is the parable, or metaphorical story.

Going down a river

Language focus	Listening
Proposed MI focus	The students "translate" from kinaesthetic–spatial to visual–spatial
Level	Upper intermediate to advanced
Time	15–20 minutes
Preparation	Be ready to read the guided fantasy slowly and fluently.

in class

1 Tell the class they are going to relax and listen to the journey of a fresh-water crab down a riverbed. As they listen to the crab's experiences, they are to imagine themselves walking along down the bank of the same river enjoying their own visual, human experiences.

2 Ask the learners to relax. Read slowly and fluently. Leave longish pauses when you come to "..." to give the students time to process what you are saying. Speak the words slowly and use the deeper part of your voice. Speed up only when the text demands it.

A Crab's Journey

I can feel the sand and pebbles under my claws and I could stay here for a long time ... The water is flowing gently round me and ... I push off from the bottom with my claws ...

Wow, now I am moving faster downstream now ... The water is swirling past me and changing speed all the time ... First fast ... then slow ... then fast again ... round a rock ... and ... BUMP BUMP ... into another one.

I seem to be in a big volume of water ... moving fast and firmly ... downstream ... Sometimes I'm skimming over the stones on the bottom ... and then the water round me wells up and I am just below the surface ... there ... with one claw out of the water ... The water round me slows and lurches forwards ...

Aaaaaah ... I'm falling ... down, down, down ... with a curtain of water round me ... THUD THUMP thank God that rock had deep moss all over it ... or I'd've smashed my shell. .....

It's different down here ... really different I mean there's lots of stuff hanging in the water ... and I am going round ... in big, slow circles ... a good feeling after that careering over the waterfall ... a really good feeling ...

And the current ... it is so slow it is hardly a flow at all. ... The current seems to be carrying me in great half circles ... first to the right and then ... to the left ... The water is ... different now ... heavier ... and full of stuff ... it tastes soily ...

Yuk ... grrr – aaaah – I can taste something really horrible. ... What is it? ... and now the water is going backwards ... what's happening? ... Where am I going? ... the taste is foul ... this water is salty ... go for the bank ... climb out ...

Ask them either to get into pairs to tell each other a bit about what they saw and felt, or to stay solo in their intrapersonal mood. If they choose to do that, they could write something about the experience that only they will see, or that they will stick on the wall for others to read. Or those who want to work quietly could join you in a corner of the room and work on river vocabulary like *pool*, *rocks*, *waterfall*, *meander*, *tidal*, *boulder*, etc.

Note

You will notice that in the above text there are some words that not all students will know. If you read the passage slowly, rhythmically and dramatically, the students' overall comprehension will be better than if they were to read the words from a page.

The text is designed to draw the learners into feeling the situation from the crab's kinaesthetic understanding of the environment, but their task is to "translate" this into human visual terms.

For more experimental exercises in the sensory area, see *Unlocking Self-expression through NLP*, Judith Baker, 2005, Delta Books.

A road not taken

Language focus	Listening, writing
Proposed MI focus	Intrapersonal and spatial
Level	Lower intermediate to advanced
Time	20–40 minutes
Preparation	Be ready to read the guided fantasy (below).

in class

1 Ask the students to relax in their chairs. Tell them to shut their eyes and to notice how they are breathing.

2 Leave them in silence for about 20 seconds, and then tell them the guided fantasy that follows. Leave longish pauses at the end of each line.

You are going to set out on a journey, quite a long journey.
This is an overland journey.

You can choose any animal or vehicle to ride on or in.
Now you are setting out on the journey – notice how it feels.
Look at the landscape either side of you.
Look at the landscape way ahead.
Notice the sort of road, track or path you are going along.

You come to a place where a way turns off to the left.
You think about this turning but you decide against taking it.
You continue your journey until nightfall.
You spend the night in a place near the road.
Next day you continue on your way.
Finally you reach the sea and can go no further.

3 Once you have brought people gently back from their trip, ask them to do two things:

• take coloured pens and draw anything they want, and
• write a page about the road to the left that they did not take.

Make it clear that this drawing and writing is private – they will not be asked to share with anybody.

Note
There is huge power in using L2 for purely private purposes. It helps students to identify better with the foreign language.

Acknowledgement
We learnt this activity in a psychosynthesis workshop.

A correspondence with oneself

Language focus   Private writing

Proposed MI focus   Intrapersonal

Level   Post beginner to advanced

Time   Each week over a term: 15 minutes
Last lesson: 45 minutes

Preparation   Each week have one envelope ready per student.
In the last week of term you will find yourself taking several letters for each student into your class.

in class

All lessons except the last

1 For 15 minutes once or twice a month, students write a letter to themselves, to be read in the last week of term. Explain that no one other than the writer will get to read their letter. What they write about is entirely up to them, but we suggest they should try to choose things that they will enjoy reading about when they read their letters. Tell them to write entirely in English. Tell them to put the time, the day of the week and the date at the top of each letter.

Tell them to write:

Dear + own name

Tell them to remember to sign the letter.

2 Give each student an envelope and ask them to write their own name on it. When the letters have been written and the envelopes named and sealed, take them in and keep them till the last week of term.

Last lesson

1 Give them time to read their own letters and then have a whole-class feedback discussion.

Round this off by asking them to write you a feedback letter – this will allow the shy ones the time they need.

Note

For once, students can write English freely, without having to worry about the teacher's corrections. You gain 15 minutes once or twice a month during which the learners are gainfully employed and during which you can relax.

Acknowledgement

Letters, Burbidge *et al*, 1996, OUP.

64

Inner grammar games

Language focus	Word order
Proposed MI focus	Intrapersonal, linguistic, and logical–mathematical
Level	Post-beginner to intermediate
Time	5–15 minutes
Preparation	Decide on the sentences to use with your students.

in class

1 Ask the class to close their eyes and relax. Explain that you are going to give them a short sentence and that you want them to *hear* it six or seven times in your voice and then *hear* it six or seven times as if their own voice was saying it.

Give them this utterance:

Well, yes, it's true ...

Leave time for them to hear the sentence in their head six or seven times – and then six or seven times again.

Tell them to now *say* it seven times in their own voices, but silently and without any physical muscle movement.

Now ask them to move the first word, *Well*, to the end of the sentence, and to say the sentence several times without muscle movement to see if it makes sense and is grammatically OK (with the right intonation, *Yes, it's true ... well ...* is fine).

Now ask them to move the new first word, *Yes*, to the end of the sentence and once again to silently try it out.

Finally *true* goes to the end again.

2 Ask the students for feedback on how well they managed to follow your instructions and on how they felt about the activity. They may also have questions about the language they were working on.

3 Do the same exercise with this sentence:

Do you want to eat now?
(The only un-OK transformation is: *to eat now, do you want?)*

Note
This inner grammar work is something students need to get used to. To do it, they have to develop new skills. We have found that doing inner grammar work in regular, short bursts makes good sense. The active attentive state while they work differs from most other moods we have felt in EFL classrooms.

Acknowledgement
We learnt the technique laid out above from several Adrian Underhill workshops. His expression for this kind of learning is "Inner Workbench".

Inner pronunciation practice

Language focus	Phonology, voice pitch, stress and intonation
Proposed MI focus	Intrapersonal, linguistic and musical.
Level	Beginner to advanced (with beginners, give the instructions in L1)
Time	5–15 minutes
Preparation	None.

in class

1 Ask the students to sit comfortably, close their eyes and relax.

2 Now give these instructions:

I am going to say a single word. **Hear** *it in your mind in my voice six or seven times.*
(pause)

Wednesday
(pause)

Now hear it in your mind in your own voice. **Hear** *it six times.*
(pause)

Wednesday
(pause)

Please **say** *it in my voice six times, but silently and with no muscle movement.*

Please **say** *it in your own voice several times, silently and with no muscle movement.*

Say *the word in your own voice,* **with** *muscle movement but still without sound.*

Whisper *the word.*

Say *the word quietly to yourself.*

Say *the word normally to a neighbour.*

Sing *the word.*

Note
Students gradually get better and better at doing this sort of activity. They need to have several chances to try it out, as you are introducing them to a whole new way of using their speech-circuits in their brain, and their vocal apparatus. Some exercises in this book are rightly one-offs. This one isn't.

Acknowledgement
We learnt this technique in a workshop given by Adrian Underhill.

Fifteen minutes of yesterday

Language focus	Past-tense verbs for naming feelings, thoughts and actions
Proposed MI focus	Intrapersonal and interpersonal. This exercise is so wide open that other intelligences are very often used
Level	Lower intermediate to advanced
Time	30–45 minutes
Preparation	None.

in class

1 Ask your students to close their eyes and count their next 15 breaths. (This helps to put them into a "going inside" mood.)

2 Tell the students to pick any short period from their memories of the previous day, and to write down 20 distinctively different things that they felt, thought or did during that period. Tell them to stay within the short period chosen or, if they don't remember it well enough, to change it to another brief period. Make clear that you are there to help with any words they may need during their writing.

3 Pair the students. Each student takes it in turn to tell their partner the starting and finishing time of their period and three of the 20 things they have written down. The other person may not ask any questions, but then guesses/intuits six more things, without either partner speaking. Both partners then write down their six guesses simultaneously.

4 The pairs share their six guesses and their 20 sentences.

5 Whole-class feedback on the exercise.

CHAPTER 5
SELF-MANAGEMENT

Excellence in language learning

Language focus   Speaking and listening

Proposed MI focus   Intrapersonal and interpersonal

Level   Intermediate upwards

Time   30–40 minutes

Preparation   None.

in class

1 Ask students to have pen and paper ready, as they are going to work individually for a period of about 20 minutes. They should try to let go of any contact with the others, and tap into a state that allows them to focus on themselves alone.

2 Ask the students to think of a moment of "peak performance" in using a foreign language. This could be any time when they used the language successfully, e.g. when talking to someone, understanding someone who spoke rather fast, reading a book or a challenging article, writing a text etc.

You may have learners in your class who don't believe they have ever done well in a language-related situation. Ask them to think of someone they know who is really good at language, and to imagine themselves becoming this person for a few minutes.

3 Ask them to remember that time as vividly as possible. Encourage them to relive the experience as if they were in it right now.

4 Read out to them the sets of questions below, one after the other. All the questions should be answered from their state of re-living the experience of being successful in the foreign language. Pause for a minute or so after each question, so that they have enough time to reflect on their answers and note them on a piece of paper.

Where are you here in this special moment in your life?
What can you see around you?
Who else is with you?
What room/space are you in?
What colours can you see?
What time of day is it?
What are you doing here in this special moment in your life?

In the next three, describe all your actions in detail:

What capabilities do you have here?
What are you at ease with?
How exactly are you using the language here?
What beliefs do you have here?
What do you think of your language-learning capabilities?
What do you think about yourself?
Why are you doing what you are doing here?
And why are you so successful in this situation?

Find a metaphor that expresses best who you are here:
If you were to choose a symbol of who you are here in this situation of success, what would you choose: a certain animal, a flower, a building?

5 Ask your students to work in small groups or in pairs. Encourage them to talk about their findings.

Acknowledgement

This exercise is influenced by what we learnt from Diana Whitmore, the author of *Psychosynthesis in Education*, and the concept of logical levels created by Robert Dilts, based on the teachings of Gregory Bateson.

Seeing a difficulty/challenge from a different perspective

Language focus	Reading comprehension, note-making
Proposed MI focus	Spatial and intrapersonal
Level	Intermediate upwards
Time	20–30 minutes
Preparation	Make a photocopy of the instructions below, one copy per student.

in class

1 Ask your students to think of something they find a bit difficult to cope with at the moment.

2 Ask them to relax and allow themselves to put that challenge or problem to the back of their minds for the time being.

3 Give each student a copy of the following instructions. Ask them to read the text first. If necessary, go through it sentence by sentence together with your class, clarifying any language questions they might have. Tell them that they will have about 15 minutes to read the text slowly, pausing after each instruction, and then to go into an intrapersonal mode and follow the instructions.

Remember one of the most beautiful landscapes you have ever seen. Imagine that you are in that landscape now. See, hear, feel and smell it as vividly as possible.

Focus on the colours and shapes you can see. Is there a blue sky? Are there any clouds? Can you see any plants or trees? How many shades of green are there? What's the distant line of the horizon like? Enjoy the beauty of the scenery.

Imagine that some of the people who you like a lot are with you in this landscape. Enjoy the feeling of being with them. Become aware of what these people mean to you.

Listen to the natural sounds of the beautiful scenery.

Allow yourself to fully enjoy the scenery and become aware of the feelings in your heart.

4 Now, in the following way, ask the students to visualise the problem they were thinking of previously:
Now put your problem into the landscape. Pay attention to your feelings for the beauty of the landscape. If any of your feelings – or the sounds, or the colours, or the smells – lose their quality, put the problem aside. Focus again on the beauty of the landscape you are in.
As soon as you can recapture the beauty of the scenery, put your problem back in again. If you are able to keep your positive inner state, leave the problem there.

© Helbling Languages 2005. Please photocopy this page for use in class.

Now allow yourself to become aware how your perception of the problem changes in the scenario of beauty and positive feelings.
Pay attention to any spontaneous solution or solutions you might find to the problem.

5 Ask your students to "come back" to the classroom, but stay "with themselves" (keeping the state of turning their attention inwards) for a few minutes. Ask them to notice how their perception of the problem has changed during the activity and to make notes of their observations. Ask them to decide on any action plan that they may want to develop, based on what they have observed.

Note

There are times when your students may feel overwhelmed, e.g. when they have to study a lot of information for a difficult test, or when they feel homesick (as can happen when they are taking a language course far from home). In such situations, it helps to get the students out of their negative, "can't do" mood by offering them an alternative way of feeling. From the perspective of the new mood, the previously looming problem will often shrink to manageable size.

Acknowledgement

We learnt this exercise from page 44 of *Pleasure in Problem Solving from the NLP Perspective*, Luis Jorge Gonzales, 1995, Editorial Font SA, Monterrey, NL, Mexico.

© Helbling Languages 2005. Please photocopy this page for use in class.

The story of your hopes and dreams

Language focus	Creative writing, speaking and listening
Proposed MI focus	Linguistic, interpersonal and intrapersonal
Level	Intermediate upwards
Time	Lesson 1: 30–40 minutes Lesson 2 (a week later): 10 minutes
Preparation	You need one envelope per student. Prepare to give a short account of a book, story or film you liked as a child.

in class

Lesson 1

1 Ask your students to make a list of dreams they have, or objectives they want to reach in their lives. Get them to underline the one dream/objective they feel most strongly about.

2 The students take a blank piece of paper. Tell them to write their dream/objective in the centre of the page and circle it. Get them to jot down in the form of a mind map all associations that come to mind.

Example:

spend a year in Australia

go to university

pass driving test:

my dreams

learn scuba diving

Study abroad

highway number 1/ Harley Davidson

3 Ask your students to put their mind maps aside. Tell them about a book you liked as a child. Give them a short summary of that book, and elaborate on why that book was important for you. Tell them also how you remember it now, e.g. what images, sounds, feelings, thoughts, words, smells, tastes etc you associate with the memory.

4 Ask your students to think of a book – or a story, or a film – that they liked when they were children. Ask them to take a few minutes for that, and to close their eyes if they like.

5 Ask them to go back to their mind maps and add ideas from the book (story/film) to them.

6 Get your students to write an imaginative story based on their mind map, starting with "Once upon a time ..."

7 When the students have finished writing, give them an envelope each. Ask them to put their story in their envelope and seal it, then write their name on the envelope. Tell the class that you are going to give them back their own envelopes in a week's time, and then collect all the envelopes.

Lesson 2

A week later, give each student their envelope. Ask them read their story silently and then to share, in small groups or in pairs, their thoughts about their stories and experience.

Note

This exercise is based on the idea that a positive past experience can induce a mood of self-confidence when facing the present and future. For example, a student re-experiencing a sports success in their mind can help them get into the right mood to do their best in an English exam.

70 Learning to be your own watchdog

Language focus Writing, self-correction and peer-correction

Proposed MI focus Linguistic, logical–mathematical, intrapersonal and, in Lesson 3, interpersonal

Level Intermediate upwards

Time Three consecutive lessons, each of 20 minutes

Preparation Select any text-writing activity you want to do with your students. Have an A4 envelope ready.

in class

Lesson 1

1 Set your class a writing task. Ask them to produce a first draft, which means that they should not worry about the accuracy or neatness of their writing. Tell them also that you are not going to read their texts. As a result, they should get into a writing flow that allows them to write without being critical of what they are producing.

2 When they have finished writing, ask them to sign their texts. Then ask a student who is trusted by the others to collect all the texts and put them into an A4 envelope and seal it. Ask the student to keep the envelope and bring it along to the next lesson.

3 As homework for the next lesson, ask the students to write another draft of the same text.

Lesson 2

1 Hand out the texts written in Lesson 1. Ask the students to read their first drafts and underline all the things in their texts that they are happy with. They should then do the same thing with the draft they wrote as homework.

2 Tell the students to produce a third draft based on what they have underlined in drafts 1 and 2, including any new ideas generated since. Make it clear to them that these texts will be shared.

Lesson 3

1 Put the students into groups of three or four. They read out their texts to each other, or exchange them and read them silently. Tell them to point out to each other parts of the texts that are not clear or could be improved in any other way.

2 The students now individually write a fourth draft of the texts, trying to improve their writing on the basis of the feedback they have received.

3 Ask them to identify any parts in their texts that they are not happy with, and come up with questions to you. Answer these questions and encourage them to write a final draft.

Acknowledgement
We learnt this technique from an article by Philip Jay Lewitt, "How to Cook a Tasty Essay", in *English Teaching Forum*, January 1990.

71 Dealing with writing blocks

Language focus	Overcoming writing blocks
Proposed MI focus	Intrapersonal and linguistic
Level	Intermediate upwards
Time	20–25 minutes
Preparation	Each student will need a piece of A4 paper.
Note	Quite a number of students have negative beliefs about their own competence in writing. Writers' blocks are often the result of negative experiences with writing, in which the focus was on accuracy only, so that the students never explored their own potential to be creative. The activity offers a stimulating and enjoyable ritual that can help students to overcome writing blocks and release their creativity. Similar rituals are used with great success in the helping professions. The activity can be great fun for the students, provided it is carried out in an atmosphere of trust that allows for humour.

in class

1 Ask your students to think of something (an object, an activity, a place etc) that gives them a lot of positive energy. Ask them to write down a word that stands for this source of energy on a slip of paper. Collect all the slips of paper in a box.

2 Walk round and ask each student to draw one folded piece of paper out of the box. Ask them to leave it folded up, and not to look at it for the time being.

3 Give your student an example of a ritual in which a figure made of wool, straw, paper or the like is burnt. Such rituals, like the Guy Fawkes bonfires in England, or the burning of Zozobra in New Mexico, have symbolic meaning. They stand for "getting rid of the evil". Ask your students for further examples they know of, and discuss the symbolic meaning of these rituals.

4 Tell your students that you are going to carry out a similar ritual with them. It is completely up to them whether they want to take it seriously or do it just for fun. You may want to tell them that such activities usually are effective even if someone is not really convinced they will help, as long as the person acts as if they believed in their power.

Tell them that lots of people have writing problems because of negative beliefs or feelings they have about their own ability to write. You may want to give them one or two examples of such beliefs, such as: *I am not a creative person.* or *I have problems expressing myself clearly in English.*

5 Hand out an A4 piece of paper to each student. Ask them to draw a Guy Fawkes figure and write their own negative beliefs on the page. Ask them to crumble their sheets of paper up. Give them a signal (*1– 2 – 3 – Go!*) and they throw their paper into a corner of the classroom.

6 Ask them to unfold the slip of paper they have drawn from the box, and to start writing a piece of text related to the word that they find there. Tell them that they should write for two minutes without stopping, and that while they are writing they should not bother about mistakes, allowing themselves to get into a flow where it does not matter if their writing is good or not. Tell them that if any critical thought comes into their head, they should include it in their writing, in this way staying in their flow all the time. Tell them that nobody is going to read their texts afterwards.

7 Finally, when the students have finished writing their pieces of texts, ask them to work with a partner and share their feelings and thoughts about the activity.

Note

You may want to tell your students that they should not worry about creating a mess in the classroom since you will tidy it up afterwards without reading anyone's notes. Remind them that the more "seriously" they take the ritual, in terms of imagining that they are really getting rid of these blocks by throwing their papers away, the better it is likely to work for them.

Students have often commented after doing this activity that they were really surprised about both the length and the quality of the text that they have produced in the two minutes' writing time.

Acknowledgement

We got the idea for this activity from the book *Anybody Can Write, A Playful Approach: Ideas for the Aspiring Writer, the Beginner, the Blocked Writer* by Roberta Jean Bryant, 1999, New World Library.

Positive language learning affirmations

Language focus	Dictation, writing
Proposed MI focus	Intrapersonal and interpersonal
Level	Intermediate upwards
Time	30–40 minutes
Preparation	None.

in class

1 Ask your class if they know what placebos are. Tell them that there are studies that show that placebos have the (perhaps surprisingly) high healing effect of over 30 per cent. This is in spite of the fact that from a purely chemical point of view, placebos should not make any difference at all. Ask them to share stories about someone they know who is a very positive thinker, even in situations that are difficult.

2 Elicit from your class in what ways positive beliefs can support language learning.

3 Dictate the following positive-belief statements. Tell your students to change them from second person to first person singular as they write the sentences down. They can also change the wording of the statements and thus change their content as long as they keep the positive quality of them:

You learnt your mother tongue.
Therefore, you have the ability to learn any foreign language you want to learn.
You are becoming more and more fluent in English.
You can understand another person and express yourself more easily in this foreign language if you focus on the communication and on the other person, not on the language.

At this point, give them a two-minute pause, and ask them to add two or three positive beliefs of their own choice. Then continue with your dictation:

It is natural and OK to make mistakes. Mistakes are a sign of learning.
You can allow yourself to enjoy language learning and develop positive feelings toward the language you are learning.
You can trust that you are learning the foreign language consciously and unconsciously.
Learning a foreign language is a process that has stages.
It makes sense to give yourself the time you need to achieve your goals.

4 Students work in pairs. (For this description, A is male and B is female.) A gives B the sheet of paper with the belief statements he has written down. A closes his eyes, B slowly reads out the first statement from the beliefs that A has added to his list. A repeats it by saying it to himself, internally. Tell them that after each statement there should be about half a minute's time for reflection. Ask them to stay "with themselves", in their inner world, and that there will be time for sharing later. (This might be an important announcement for people who have a need to communicate with others all the time.)

5 When B has finished reading A's statements, they swap roles.

6 Ask the pairs to share between them the effect that hearing and repeating the positive belief statements has had on each of them. Ask them to discuss which of the belief statements are easier to take on board than others.

Note

According to research done by Robert Dilts, the three main negative beliefs people sometimes have are:

I can't do it

It's not possible

I don't deserve it or *I'm not worth it.*

It is common sense that students who perceive themselves to be good learners of a foreign language will be more successful at learning one than someone who has a belief that they are hopeless when it comes to language learning. This exercise is aimed at helping students to build up positive language-learning beliefs through affirmations, a technique widely used by, for example, sports professionals.

Acknowledgement

The format of this activity was influenced by an activity we learnt from Robert Dilts, the author of *Changing Belief Systems with NLP*, 1990, Meta Publications, Cupertino CA.

73 Imaginary (or intuitive) walk

Language focus	Speaking and listening
Proposed MI focus	Interpersonal and intrapersonal
Level	Intermediate upwards
Time	30–40 minutes
Preparation	Think of a story to tell your class in which your subconscious played an important role, or about an intuition you had.

Here is an example:

My flight was boarding, and I was not allowed to take my hand luggage into the aircraft. I had to put it on a trolley, and the attendant told me that it would be handed back to me immediately after landing. At the top of the steps, just as I was about to get on the plane, I saw a picture of my car keys in my mind's eye. Without thinking, I turned round and walked back down to where my case was. They were just about to load it onto the aircraft, and I managed to stop the procedure. I took out the car keys and went back onto the plane.

After we had landed there was no sign of my bag. Thank goodness, I at least had my car keys on me and so could get home.

---

in class

1 Tell the story you have prepared and ask your class to share similar stories.

2 Announce that you will ask them to imagine that they are going for walks individually. Give them the following three questions and make sure they understand them as metaphorical and not geographical:

   Where am I (in my present development)?
   Where do I want to go?
   What do I need in order to get there?

3 Tell them that they have roughly 20 minutes for their imaginary walk. Ask them to "switch off" their rational thinking as much as possible, and let themselves be guided by their intuition. Tell them to meditate on the first question above, and allow themselves to intuitively think of an object that somehow symbolises the answer to the question. Tell them that they should not select something consciously, but trust their intuitive feelings to select the object for them. They should also not judge the object critically, even if the choice comes as a total surprise to them. Ask them to carry on like this with the other two questions, and then make a drawing of the three objects.

4 Put the students into groups of three. They present their drawings of their objects to each other, without revealing what the drawings symbolise for them.

5 When everybody has presented their drawings, the members of the group talk about positive qualities they believe the different objects symbolically have.

6 If students want, they can then share what the objects symbolise for them and how they felt during the exercise.

Note

If you are working with adult students and there is space, you can ask students to go on real walks and look for the objects. Again, they should not 'consciously' select objects, but let themselves be guided by their intuition.

Students could possibly also bring some of the objects to class – but if that is not possible, again get them to draw their objects.

74

Problem-solving patterns

Language focus	Writing and speaking
Proposed MI focus	Logical–mathematical and other intelligences
Level	Intermediate upwards
Time	40–50 minutes
Preparation	None.

in class

1 Ask each student to think of two problems they have successfully solved in the last few weeks. Tell them that they have 10 minutes to note down exactly HOW they managed to solve the problems. Ask them to focus on the steps they went through in order to solve each problem. Do not give them any examples at this point.

2 Ask your students to work in groups of three or four. Get them to tell each other briefly about the problems they had, and to share their findings about how they solved the problems. The other members of the group should ask questions in order to be able to compare and contrast different ways used by different people to solve their problems.

3 Get each group to draw a diagram or flow chart for each different approach to solving a problem that they have found in the group.

4 Get each group to present to the class the different problem-solving approaches found in each group. They should not elaborate on the content of the problem, but merely on HOW the problems were solved.

5 As they make their presentations, list on the board the different ways of solving a problem that they have come up with, and get them to give each different way a catchy name.

Note

This is an adaptation of an exercise in David Lazear's book *Seven Pathways of Learning*, 1994, Zephyr Press.

Teacher's quick-reference guide

To use the chart on pages 157-158, decide on the lesson-time available to you, and find it in the left-hand column. Then look across the grid till you reach the column showing the standard of your students. (Or start with your students and work down to the time.)

Any filled cell you reach gives you a suitable recipe number.
And in that same row, the cell in the right-hand column indicates the proposed MI focus.

Beginner	Post-Beginner	Elementary	Lower Int.	Intermediate	Upper Int.	Advanced	MI focus
			20	20	20	20	logical–mathematical
			24	24			logical–mathematical, linguistic
27	27	27	27	27	27	27	linguistic, kinaesthetic
			28	28	28	28	linguistic, musical
43	43	43	43	43	43	43	interpersonal, linguistic
			49	49	49		intrapersonal, interpersonal
			58	58	58	58	linguistic, spatial
		59	59	59	59		intrapersonal, interpersonal, linguistic
	25	25	25	25	25		interpersonal, linguistic
			45	45	45		logical–mathematical, linguistic, spatial
		60	60	60	60		intrapersonal, interpersonal
64	64	64	64				intrapersonal, logical–mathematical, linguistic
65	65	65	65	65	65	65	intrapersonal, linguistic, musical
						5	linguistic, musical
32	32	32	32	32			logical–mathematical, spatial
		36	36	36	36	36	interpersonal
						38	logical–mathematical, linguistic
			44	44	44	44	intrapersonal, interpersonal
			52	52	52	52	interpersonal, musical
			55	55	55		linguistic, spatial, kinaesthetic
					61	61	spatial, kinaesthetic
				13			spatial
				71	71	71	intrapersonal, linguistic
				5	5		linguistic, musical
						11	logical–mathematical
				16	16	16	logical–mathematical, spatial
				17	17	17	logical–mathematical, spatial
		18	18	18	18	18	All
		19	19	19	19	19	All
	22	22	22	22	22	22	interpersonal, linguistic, spatial, kinaesthetic
	23	23	23	23	23	23	logical–mathematical
			33	33	33	33	musical, spatial, kinaesthetic
		34	34	34	34	34	linguistic, musical, kinaesthetic
	40	40	40	40			intrapersonal, interpersonal, linguistic
			46	46	46	46	logical–mathematical, spatial
				51			logical–mathematical, spatial
			53	53	53	53	logical–mathematical, spatial
	54	54	54	54			intrapersonal, interpersonal, logical–mathematical

Beginner	Post-Beginner	Elementary	Lower Int.	Intermediate	Upper Int.	Advanced	MI focus
				68	68	68	intrapersonal, spatial
			2	2	2	2	intrapersonal, interpersonal
				4	4	4	logical–mathematical, linguistic
	5	5	5				linguistic, musical
					9		interpersonal, logical–mathematical
				10			All
				12			All
			21	21	21	21	linguistic, spatial, kinaesthetic
				35	35	35	intrapersonal, interpersonal
			37				linguistic
	41	41	41	41			interpersonal, logical–mathematical, linguistic, and musical / spatial
			42	42	42	42	intrapersonal, interpersonal, logical–mathematical
			48	48			intrapersonal, interpersonal, logical–mathematical
		56	56	56	56	56	interpersonal
			62	62	62	62	intrapersonal, spatial
				67	67	67	intrapersonal, interpersonal
				72	72	72	intrapersonal, interpersonal
				73	73	73	intrapersonal, interpersonal
				39	39	39	logical–mathematical, kinaesthetic
			66	66	66	66	intrapersonal, interpersonal, plus others
			3	3	3	3	musical, kinaesthetic
				6	6	6	linguistic
	30	30	30	30	30	30	musical, kinaesthetic
	31	31	31	31			interpersonal, spatial
				74	74	74	logical–mathematical and others
7	7	7	7	7	7	7	intrapersonal, kinaesthetic
				47	47	47	linguistic
			26	26			interpersonal, linguistic
			57	57	57	57	linguistic, spatial
		15	15				logical–mathematical, spatial
	50	50	50	50	50	50	kinaesthetic
			29	29	29	29	spatial
				69	69	69	intrapersonal, interpersonal, linguistic
			1	1	1	1	All
				8	8	8	intrapersonal, interpersonal, + any
				14	14	14	All
				70	70	70	intrapersonal, interpersonal, logical–mathematical, linguistic
	63	63	63	63	63	63	intrapersonal